PRECAUTIONS TO AVOID POSSIBLE EXPOSURE TO EXCESSIVE MICROWAVE ENERGY

(a) **DO NOT** attempt to operate this oven with the door open since open-door operation can result in harmful exposure to microwave energy. It is important not to defeat or tamper with the safety interlocks.

(b) **DO NOT** place any object between the oven front face and the door or allow soil or cleaner residue to accumulate on sealing surfaces.

(c) **DO NOT** operate the oven if it is damaged. It is particularly important that the oven door close properly and that there is no damage to the: (1) Door (bent), (2) hinges and latches (broken or loosened), (3) door seals and sealing surfaces.

(d) The oven should **NOT** be adjusted or repaired by anyone except properly qualified service personnel.

 WARNING

To avoid personal injury or property damage, observe the following:

1. Briskly stir or pour liquids before heating to prevent spontaneous boiling or eruption. Do not overheat. If air is not mixed into a liquid, liquid can erupt in oven or after removal from oven.

2. Do not heat sealed containers or plastic bags in oven. Containers with restricted openings such as syrup bottles or baby food jars must not be used for cooking. Food or liquid could expand quickly and cause container or bag to break. Pierce or open container or bag before heating.

 Caution

To avoid personal injury or property damage, observe the following:

1. Always press STOP/RESET before programming oven.

2. Do not deep fat fry in oven. Fat could overheat and be hazardous to handle.

3. Do not cook or reheat eggs in shell or with an unbroken yolk. Pressure may buildup and erupt. Pierce yolk with a fork or knife before cooking. Do not reheat previously cooked eggs in the microwave oven unless finely chopped or scrambled.

4. Pierce skin of potatoes, tomatoes, or other foods with a "skin" before cooking in microwave oven. This allows steam to escape during cooking.

5. Remove excess fat from meats and poultry to prevent spattering.

6. Do not heat baby bottles in microwave oven.

7. Do not home can in microwave oven. Home canning is generally done with metal lids. Since metal lids reflect heat, product may not be heated uniformly to 212°F or above. Food could deteriorate. USDA extension specialists do not recommend home canning in microwave ovens.

8. All uncooked foods should be heated to a final internal temperature of at least 165°F. Some foods require higher temperatures. These recommended temperatures kill most food borne, disease causing organisms. Some common visual signs that indicate the cooking temperature has been reached:
   • Food steams throughout, not just around edges.
   • Center bottom of dish is very hot to the touch.

9. If using a microwave popcorn popper, use according to manufacturer's instructions. Do not continue to heat after popping has stopped. Popcorn will scorch or burn. Do not leave oven unattended.

10. Use only popcorn in packages designed and labeled for microwave use. Pop according to package directions, beginning with the minimum amount of time recommended. Use caution when handling hot popcorn bag.

In Short Order

**A Cook's Companion to Microwave
and Convection Cooking**

Contents

Introduction

YOUR NEW MICRO-CONVECTION OVEN combines the most advanced cooking options available today. In one compact appliance you can microwave; convection; or combination cook with microwave and convection energy. Defrosting frozen foods and keeping cooked foods warm are other tasks your oven will perform too, if so programmed.

In addition to these basic procedures, using the cooking modes in sequence will add yet other dimensions to your cooking vocabulary. For example, in Onion Soup Gratinée, the onions are cooked with microwave energy, then the top is baked in the convection mode for a lightly browned finish.

All of these options make your oven the most sophisticated and versatile piece of cooking equipment in your kitchen. To realize its fullest potential, review the owner's manual. It contains precise directions for its operations.
The introduction to micro-convection cooking, the meal preparation techniques, and tne recipes which follow are intended to complement these instructions and to get you started cooking, in short order...and with the most delicious results.

What Is Micro-convection Cooking?

To understand micro-convection cooking, one has to look at each method separately. Not only does your oven function differently when set for each cooking cycle, but each has different uses in your cooking repertoire.

Microwave cooking uses the energy of electromagnetic waves, which are shorter but similar to radio waves, to cook food.
Electromagnetic waves are transmitted by a magnetron tube to the oven's cavity where they bounce off its metal walls and are absorbed by the food. Microwaves entering the food, cook by vibrating its molecules, causing friction and subsequently heat. Microwaves penetrate food to a maximum depth of 1 $\frac{1}{2}$ inches, depending on the density of the food. As a result, the interior of thicker foods, such as roasts, are cooked by heat conducted from the outside layer.

The virtues of microwave cooking have been extolled by many a cook. It is fast. It saves energy. The microwave oven is easy to operate, even for children. Cooking with microwave energy does not require as much fat and water, resulting in more nutritiously prepared food. Among the wide-ranging applications for food preparation, microwaves steam vegetables and fish to perfection. The microwave oven is un-paralleled at reheating leftovers and preparing sauces. Cooking bacon via microwaves energy is nothing short of kitchen wizardry.

Some foods cooked with microwave energy are not as browned or crisp as when prepared by dry heat in a convectional oven. When those results are desired, use the convection or combination cooking methods as suggested in this cookbook.

Convection cooking, including baking, and roasting, can all be accomplished in your oven. Convection cooking is closest to traditional oven cooking.

Similar to a conventional, or thermal oven, a convection oven contains a heating element that generates the dry heat needed to produce crisp, brown exteriors on food. In addition, its construction also incorporates a fan to circulate the hot air in the oven cavity. Constantly circulating air within the oven creates a more uniform temperature to promote even cooking. For ease in preparation of a recipe during preheating time, assemble all ingredients before programming desired preheat temperature.

In some instances, it is convenient to bake items directly on the turntable.

Combination cooking combines the best features of both the cooking method. In this method, your oven alternately pulses convection and microwave energy, thus cooking food with the speed of microwaves without sacrificing crispness or appearance. When using the Convection rack in combination cooking, it is sometimes easier to put the cooking container on the Convection rack and place both in the microwave oven at one time. In other cases, it is more efficient to do otherwise. We have taken this into consideration with all recipes and have witten them according to what, in our judgement, is most suitable.

Cooking Containers: Microwave, Convection, and Combination Cooking

Microwave cooking containers are especially varied. Virtually everything in your kitchen cupboard, with the exception of metal or metal-trimmed containers and pots, qualifies as a cooking container. Consider microwavable paper plates and napkins, dinner plates and glass measuring cups in varying sizes, ceramic oven-to-table cookware, glass casseroles with lids, and glass baking dishes. Metal can cause arcing (a sparking, listening-like effect) in your microwave oven that you can see and hear. It can demage your oven, so avoid using metal contaiiners or metal twist ties.

Check labels on cooking utensils and products for correct usage. If in doubt about a container, perform this test:
1. Place the container in question beside a cup of water in a glass measuring cup in the oven.
2. Cook at POWER HI for 1 minute.
3. If the container gets hot, it is absorbing microwave energy and should not be used for microwave cooking. If it remains cool and only the water gets warm, the container is suitable for microwave cooking.

For convection cooking, conventional metal pans and disposable containers are fine, as are ovenproof ceramic and glass cookware.

For combination cooking use only ovenproof ceramic and glass cookware, plastic utensils desiged for both microwave energy and convection heat, or special disposable containers manufactured for microwave/thermal use. Again, follow the manufacturer's guidelines. See the Owner's manual for a detailed list of cooking containers and utensils suitable for microwave, convection, and combination cooking.

The Convection Rack and turntable are suitable for all cooking cycles.

Microwave Cooking: Techniques and Tips

To promote even cooking, select roasts that are of regular shape with no jagged edges; cut foods for stews, casseroles and soups in uniform pieces. Pierce foods with a skin (potatoes, squash) or membrane (yolk of an egg) before microwaving to prevent bursting as the food cooks.

THE SHAPE AND SIZE of container used for cooking will affect speed and evenness of cooking. The optimum cooking container is ring-shaped, as it allows microwaves to penetrate more surfaces. In general, straight-sided containers give more even results than sloping sided ones. Rounded shapes are preferable to square for the same reason. Food should fill containers comfortably, yet allow space for bubbling up, as in some soups or milk-based sauces.

SALT meats and poultry after cooking, since salt tends to cause dry spots when used before cooking.

COVERING cooking containers with plastic wrap is often recommended. Use those plastic wraps specified as microwavable and always vent one corner to minimize the buildup of steam. When removing wrap, carefully lift away from you to avoid hot steam.
Always cover a food if a moist, even heat is required. Covering not only prevents too much evaporation when a small amount of liquid is used, but it traps hot steam using its energy to cook food along with microwave energy. Covering also minimizes spattering of food. Appropriate coverings for moist cooking are microwavable lids or plastic wrap. Use waxed paper to minimize spattering; and microwavable paper towel as a covering to absorb extra moisture.

SPACING AND ARRANGING ensures even cooking. Individual foods, such as baking potatoes, should be placed in a circle around edge of turntable, with an equal amount of space between them. Place foods that are uneven in thickness, such as chicken legs, with the thickest portions toward the outside edge of the dish or Convection Rack. Arrange denser sections of vegetables (broccoli stems) in the same manner.

REARRANGE larger pieces of food in casserole or on roast rack during the cooking to ensure even results.

TURN food over during cooking to allow microwave energy to uniformly penetrate all areas.

STIRRING helps promote even cooking of liquids. Since outsides of microwaved mixtures heat first, stir from the outside towards the center to redistribute heat.

SHIELD corners of square baking pans and wing tips of chicken with small pieces of foil to prevent them from cooking too rapidly. Be sure foil molds to the surface and does not stick out away from the mass of food. Only use small amounts of foil where needed to protect against over browning. Be sure foil does not touch oven lining since arcing and damage to the magnetron tube can occur.

ELEVATING foods on a microwavable roast rack, such as bacon or kabobs, allows grease and juices to drain away from food.

STANDING TIME in a microwave recipe is part of the cooking process. Do not omit it. It allows heat in food to equalize and completes the cooking. Tent food, such as roasts, with foil or leave cooked as directed in the recipe for duration of standing time after the food is removed from the oven.

FOODS TO BE DEFROSTED can be put directly from freezer into oven if they are wrapped in freezer paper or microwavable plastic pouches. Place food, such as a roast, in a baking dish to catch juices. Remove all metal ties. Turn food over during defrosting. Chicken parts, burger patties, fish fillets, etc. will defrost faster when parts are separated.

Meal Preparation Techniques

To acquaint you with the versatility, ease of operation, and different cooking cycles (microwave, convection, and micro-convection combination) of your new oven, we've outlined three very simple meals to cook in it over the course of a day.

BREAKFAST: Everyone's in a hurry at breakfast time. But using the microwave setting, frozen orange juice and a mug of steaming hot coffee or tea can both be ready in less than 2 minutes; egg and bacon—5 minutes later. Here's how to do it.

1. To reconstitute frozen juice in a jiffy: Remove the top from a 6-ounce plastic container or frozen orange juice (if the container is foil lined, remove frozen juice block to a microwavable container.) Place frozen juice in container in center of oven on turntable. Cook at POWER 5 for 1½ to 2 minutes. Remove thawed juice concentrate, dilute with cold water as package directs, and serve.

2. For coffee and tea, place a microwavable mug or 1-cup glass measuring cup of cold water in center of oven on turntable. Cook at POWER HI for 2 minutes. Add instant coffee or tea bag to mug, or pour hot water through a filter containing freshly ground coffee or tea leaves.

3. Bacon cooked via microwaves is nothing short of a miracle! There is no hazardous hot grease to contend with and discard, no greasy pan to scour, and each piece cooks prefectly with little attention from the cook. Simply place 2 slices of bacon on double thickness of paper towel on a microwavable plate. Cover bacon with an additional layer of paper towel. Place in oven on turntable. Cook at POWER HI for 2 to 2 ½ minutes, depending on desired degree of crispness.

4. Two scrambled eggs: First melt 2 teaspoons butter in a 2-cup glass measuring cup. Cook at POWER HI for 25 to 30 seconds.
Break two eggs into the same measuring cup, add 2 tablespoons milk; beat until well blended with fork. Cook at POWER 8 for 1 minute. Break up and stir eggs with a fork. Cook at POWER 8 for 1 to 1½ minutes. Let stand covered for 1 minute.

LUNCH: Here's a lunch break that's so simple that a ten year old can fix it safely.

1. Pierce hot dog with fork. Place hot dog in bun; wrap in paper towel to absorb moisture. Cook at POWER HI for 30 to 45 seconds. Let stand 1 minute. Unwrap and eat.

2. Canned soup without a pot to wash! Combine a 10 ¾ -ounce can of condensed soup with a can of milk or water in a microwavable bowl or measuring cup. Cook at POWER 7 for 2 to 2 ½ minutes, then stir. Continue to cook at POWER 7 for 2 ½ minutes.

DINNER: Hot food in a snap and cooked to perfection no matter when family members arrive home! This is possible when you use all three cooking methods.

1. Fresh broccoli for one: Trim 4 ½ ounces of fresh broccoli discarding stem end; wash. Place in microwavable dish with stems pointing towards outside edge of dish. Sprinkle 1 tablespoon of water. Cover with microwavable plastic wrap; vent; Cook at POWER HI for 2 minutes. Let stand for 1 minute. Add a pat of butter before serving.

2. Frozen fried chicken, without sacrificing a crispy finish, is ready in 15 minutes using the combination setting on your oven. Place fried chicken parts in an 8 x 8 x 2-inch glass baking dish. Cook at COMBI HIGH for 15 minutes or until brown and crispy. Rearrange pieces halfway through cooking time.

3. Bake potatoes along with the chicken. Scrub, pierce with a fork, and place in oven 10 minutes before the chicken. Cook at COMBI HIGH for 25 minutes adding chicken to oven after 10 minutes. Use oven mitts when inserting or removing foods from oven.

4. If you like biscuits, you'll love the way they bake-browned and light-using convection method. Preheat the oven as recipe or package directs using the CONVECTION temperature setting. Bake as directed on package directly on turntable or in a metal baking pan, using oven mitts with heated oven.

5. A baked apple for dessert cooks while you are eating dinner. Peel and core a large baking apple almost through to the blossom end. Fill with brown sugar, raisins, etc., if desired. Place in a large 10-ounce dish. Sprinkle with water. Cover with microwavable plastic wrap; vent. Cook at POWER HI for 2 ½ minutes. Let stand covered for 5 minutes before serving.

6. Leftovers don't seem leftover when reheated in the microwave. Place individual portions on a microwavable plate, placing foods that are more dense near plates edge. Cover with microwavable plastic wrap; vent. For meat, vegetable, potato: Cook at POWER 8 for 2 ½ to 3 minutes.

7. Do not heat any type of baby bottles or body food in microwave oven. Uneven heating may occur and possibly cause personal injury.

Do not heat small-necked containers, such as syrup bottles, in the microwave oven.
Do use the microwave wisely to enjoy many moist, tender, nutritious foods.

Starters and Snacks

CHICKEN WINGS

1   pound chicken wings

3   tablespoons Worcestershire sauce

1   teaspoon hot pepper sauce

1   clove garlic, minced

1   tablespoon fresh lemon juice

1/4 teaspoon black pepper

    Blue cheese dip

Cut chicken wings at joint; remove tips. Combine Worcestershire sauce, pepper sauce, garlic, and lemon juice in a large mixing bowl; stir well. Add wings; toss to coat. Sprinkle with pepper. Marinate covered in refrigerator for 1 hour. Drain chicken; discard marinade. Preheat CONVECTION to 400°F. Arrange wings crosswise on Convection Rack. Place rack on turntable. Cook at CONVECTION (425°F) for 20 to 25 minutes or until fork-tender. Serve with blue cheese dip.

6 servings

PIGS IN A BLANKET

1   package (8 ounces) refrigerated crescent dinner rolls

1   pound cocktail franks or Vienna sausages

    Spicy brown mustard

Preheat CONVECTION to 375°F. Unroll dough onto light floured surface; separate in to four rectangles. Pinch seams to seal perforations. Beginning at shorter side, cut each rectangle into 12 thin strips (each about 1/2 -inch wide) with scissors. Wrap each frank with dough strip. Place 16 wrapped franks at a time in an 8×8×2-inch glass baking pan. Cook at CONVECTION (375°F) for 12 to 14 minutes or until lightly browned and throughly heated. Repeat with remaining franks. Serve with spicy brown mustard.

48 appetizers

SOUTHWEST NACHOS

1 package (8 ounces) round tortilla chips
1 can (16 ounces) refried beans
2 cups shredded Cheddar cheese
½ cup dairy sour cream
½ cup jalapeño pepper slices
4 green onions, sliced
　 Sliced radishes

Arrange 12 tortilla chips on a microwavable plate. Spread each chip with 2 teaspoons of refried beans; sprinkle with Cheddar cheese. Cook uncovered at POWER HI for 1 to 1 ½ minutes or until cheese is melted. Before serving, top each chip with ½ teaspoon sour cream and then 1 slice of jalapeño pepper. Sprinkle with green onions. Garnish with radishes. Repeat with remaining ingredients.

48 nachos

HOT ARTICHOKE DIP

1 can (14 ounces) artichoke hearts, drained, finely chopped
¾ cup grated Parmesan cheese
¾ cup mayonnaise

Combine artichoke hearts, Parmesan cheese, and mayonnaise in a 1-quart microwavable casserole; mix well. Cook covered at POWER 8 for 4 to 5 minutes or until thoroughly heated; stir once.

2 cups

CURRIED CHICKEN SKEWERS

3 tablespoons fresh orange juice
2 tablespoons pineapple preserves
1 teaspoon instant minced onion
1 teaspoon packed brown sugar
½ teaspoon curry powder
½ teaspoon grated fresh orange peel
¼ teaspoon garlic powder
¼ teaspoon ground red pepper
9 ounces boneless, skinless chicken breast, cut into ½-inch strips
2 green onions, cut into 1-inch pieces
½ cup mayonnaise
1 tablespoon dairy sour cream
¼ teaspoon curry powder

For marinade, combine orange juice, preserves, minced onion, brown sugar, curry powder, orange peel, garlic powder and red pepper in a mixing bowl. Add chicken; stir to coat. Marinate covered in refrigerator for 1 hour. Drain chicken; discard marinade. Thread one chicken strip onto wooden skewer. Place green onion at end of skewer. Repeat with remaining chicken and green onions. Arrange skewers on a microwavable roast rack in a circular pattern. Cover with waxed paper. Cook at POWER HI for 3 to 3½ minutes or until chicken is no longer pink. Let stand covered 1 to 2 minutes. Combine mayonnaise, sour cream and curry powder in a small bowl. Serve with chicken.

12 appetizers.

SKEWERED SHRIMP

1 medium red pepper, cut into 1-inch squares

1 tablespoon water

1/2 pound medium shrimp, shelled, deveined

1 can (8 ounces) whole water chestnuts, drained

3 tablespoons soy sauce

2 tablespoons white vermouth

1 tablespoon sesame oil

1/4 cup thinly sliced green onions

1 clove garlic, minced

1 tablespoon ground ginger

1/4 teaspoon black pepper

Put red pepper and water into a 2-cup glass measuring cup. Cover with plastic wrap; vent. Cook covered at POWER HI for 2 minutes; drain. Alternate red pepper, shrimp, and water chestnuts on eight 6-inch wooden skewers. Place in a shallow baking dish. Combine soy sauce, vermouth, sesame oil, green onions, garlic, ginger, and pepper; pour over skewered shrimp and vegetables. Marinate covered in refrigerator for 30 minutes. Arrange skewers on a microwavable roast rack; brush with marinade. Cook uncovered at POWER HI for 4 to 5 minutes or until shrimp are opaque. Serve immediately.

4 servings

SWISS FONDUE

1 clove garlic, cut in half

1 1/4 cups dry white wine

4 cups shredded Swiss cheese

3 tablespoons flour

1/4 teaspoon ground mace

1/8 teaspoon ground red pepper

2 tablespoons brandy

French bread cubes

Rub inside of a 2-quart microwavable casserole with cut garlic; discard garlic. Pour wine into casserole. Cook uncovered at POWER HI for 3 to 4 minutes or until wine is hot but not boiling. Meanwhile, combine Swiss cheese, flour, mace and red pepper in a large plastic food storage bag; shake to coat cheese. Stir cheese mixture into hot wine. Cook uncovered at POWER 5 for 4 to 5 minutes or until cheese is melted and mixture is smooth; stir twice. Stir in brandy. Dip French bread cubes into fondue using forks or skewers. Serve warm.

About 2 1/2 cups

BAKED STUFFED CLAMS

2 slices bacon, cut into 2-inch pieces

2 tablespoons butter or margarine

1 clove garlic, minced

1/2 cup fresh bread crumbs

1 tablespoon chopped fresh parsley

1/4 teaspoon salt

1/8 teaspoon coarsely ground black pepper

1 dozen cherrystone clams

Place bacon on a microwavable roast rack. Cover with double thickness of paper towel. Cook at MICRO POWR HI for 1 1/2 to 2 1/2 minutes. Cool and crumble; set aside. Put butter and garlic into a 1-cup glass measuring cup. Cook uncovered at POWER HI for 1 minute. Combine bread crumbs, reserved bacon, butter-garlic mixture, parsley, salt, and pepper in a small mixing bowl; mix well. Set aside. Wash and scrub clams under cold running water. Arrange six clams in a circle on a microwavable plate. Cook uncovered at POWER HI for 1 to 1 1/2 minutes or until all shells are opened. Repeat with remaining clams. When cool enough to handle, remove and discard top half of shell. Loosen clams from shells with a sharp knife. Preheat CONVECTION to 400°F. Place 1 teaspoon of seasoned bread crumb mixture on top of each clam. Arrange clams in a 10-inch glass pie plate. Cook at CONVECTION (425°F) for 9 to 10 minutes or until clams are tender and edges begin to curl. Serve immediately.

1 dozen appetizers

HAM AND LEEK GRATINÉE

4 leeks (about 2 pounds)

1 tablespoon water

   White Sauce (see recipe)

8 Slices boiled ham (about 1 ounce each)

1/2 cup shredded Swiss cheese

Trim most of green parts from leeks. Split leeks in half lengthwise and soak in very cold water for 20 minutes to remove sand. Meanwhile, prepare White Sauce as directed in recipe; set aside. Wash leeks thoroughly under running water, keeping leeks from separating into single leaves; drain. Put leeks and water into a 1 1/2-quart microwavable and ovenproof baking dish. Cover with plastic wrap; vent. Cook covered at POWER HI for 4 to 5 minutes or until leaves are just tender. Set aside to cool. Preheat CONVECTION to 400°F. Drain leeks. Wrap each leek half with one slice of ham. Return to baking dish; arrange seam side down alternating white and green ends. Top with reserved white sauce and sprinkle with cheese. Cook at CONVECTION (425°F) for 15 to 20 minutes or until hot and bubbly.

8 servings

STEAMED CLAMS IN GREEN SAUCE

2   tablespoons olive oil

2   cloves garlic, thinly sliced

1/8   teaspoon black pepper

1   dozen littleneck or cherrystone clams, scrubbed

1/2   cup coarsely chopped parsley

Hot cooked spinach or regular pasta

Combine olive oil, garlic, and pepper in a 2-quart microwavable casserole. Cook covered at POWER HI for 2 to 3 minutes or until hot. Stir in clams. Cook covered at POWER HI for 4 to 5 minutes or until clams open; stir once. Let stand covered for 3 to 4 minutes. Serve immediately over hot cooked spinach or pasta.

2 servings

GRANOLA

2   cups quick oats, uncooked

1/2   cup almonds, coarsely chopped

1/4   cup roasted sunflower seeds

1/4   cup toasted wheat germ

1/4   cup shredded, sweetened coconut

1/2   cup chopped dates

1/2   cup raisins

1/3   cup honey

1   teaspoon vanilla extract

Combine oats, almonds, sunflower seeds, wheat germ, and coconut in an 8 x 8 x 2-inch glass baking dish. Preheat CONVECTION to 400°F. Cook at CONVECTION (425°F) for 10 to 12 minutes; stir every 2 minutes. Add dates, raisins, honey, and vanilla; stir to coat. Reduce CONVECTION to 375°F. Cook at CONVECTION (375°F) for 8 to 10 minutes; stir every 2 minutes. Allow to cool completely; stir occasionally. Store in an air-tight container.

8 servings

CHICKEN LIVER PÂTÉ

1 cup diced pared apple

1/2 cup plus 2 tablespoons butter, divided.

1/4 cup thinly sliced green onions

1 pound chicken livers

1/2 cup heavy cream

1 teaspoon salt

1/4 teaspoon white pepper

Sliced Apples, Crackers, or French bread

Put apple, 2 tablespoons butter and green onions into a 2-quart microwavable casserole. Cook uncovered at POWER HI for 1 to 1 1/2 minutes or until butter is melted. Rinse chicken livers under cold water; pat dry with paper towels. Cut livers in half; pierce with a fork. Stir livers into apple mixture. Cook covered at POWER 5 for 10 to 12 minutes or until livers are cooked; stir once. Allow to cool 10 minutes. Drain off excess liquid. Purée liver mixture in a blender or food processor, adding remaining 1/2 cup butter cream alternately until mixture is smooth. Blend in salt and pepper. Pour mixture into a 1-quart serving container. Chill covered for 2 to 3 hours or until completely set. Serve with sliced apples, crackers or French bread.

2 1/2 cups

STUFFED MUSHROOM CAPS

8 ounces fresh medium mushrooms (about 15 mushrooms)

2 tablespoons butter or margarine

2 tablespoons sliced green onion

1 tablespoon brandy

1/4 cup herb and garlic cheese spread

2 tablespoons dry bread crumbs

2 tablespoons finedly chopped pecans

1 tablespoon chopped fresh parsley

Clean mushrooms by wiping with damp paper towels. Remove stems; set caps aside. Finely chop stems. Put butter and green onion into a 1-quart glass measuring cup. Cook uncovered at POWER HI for 1 to 1 1/2 minutes or until butter is melted. Add chopped mushrooms and brandy; mix well. Cook uncovered at POWER HI for 3 minutes; stir once. Add cheese spread, bread crumbs, pecans, and parsley; mix well. Spoon stuffing mixture into mushroom caps. Place mushroom caps on paper towel-lined microwavable plate. Cook uncovered at POWER HI for 3 to 4 minutes or until mushrooms are tender.

About 15 appetizers

Soups

ORIENTAL CHICKEN SOUP

1/2	cup diced carrots
1	tablespoon butter or margarine
2	cans (14-1/2 ounces) beef broth
2	cups shredded iceberg lettuce
1	cup diced cooked chicken
2	tablespoons soy sauce
1/4	teaspoon ground ginger
1/8	teaspoon garlic powder
1/8	teaspoon seasame oil
1	green onion, thinly sliced

Put carrots and butter into a 2-quart microwavable casserole. Cook covered at POWER HI for 2 to 3 minutes or until tender-crisp. Stir in broth, lettuce, chicken, soy sauce, ginger, garlic, and sesame oil. Cook uncovered at POWER HI for 7 to 8 minutes or until thoroughly heated; stir twice. Garnish with green onions.

4 servings

TRADITIONAL OYSTER STEW

2	cups (1 pint) half-and-half or milk
2	dozen shucked oysters, with liquor
1/4	teaspoon salt
4	teaspoons butter or margarine
	Paprika

Pour half-and-half or milk into a 1-quart glass measuring cup. Cook uncovered at POWER HI for 4 to 5 minutes or until hot but not boiling. Add oysters, liquor, and salt; stir. Cook uncovered at POWER 7 for 2 to 3 minutes or until edges of oysters curl. Ladle stew into four soup bowls; top with butter and sprinkle with paprika. Serve immediately.

4 servings

CORN AND PEPPER CHOWDER

5   slices bacon, cut into 1/2-inch pieces

1/4   cup finely chopped celery

1/4   cup finely chopped onion

1/4   cup finely chopped green pepper

1/4   cup finely chopped red pepper

2   tablespoons flour

2   cups milk

1   can (17 ounces) whole kernel corn, undrained

1   medium potato, peeled, cut into 1/2-inch cubes

1   teaspoon chopped fresh parsley

1   teaspoon chopped fresh dill or 1/2 teaspoon dried dill weed

1/4   teaspoon salt

1/8   teaspoon white pepper

    Fresh dill

Combine bacon, celery, onion, green and red pepper in a 3-quart microwavable casserole. Cook uncovered at POWER HI for 8 to 9 minutes or until bacon is crisp and vegetables are tender; stir once. Stir flour into bacon mixture.

Add milk, corn, potato, parsley, dill, salt, and white pepper; mix well. Cook covered at POWER HI for 13 to 15 minutes or until slightly thickened and potatoes are tender; stir three times. Let stand 3 minutes. Garnish with fresh dill.

4 servings

CREAM OF VEGETABLE SOUP

2   tablespoons butter or margarine

1/4   cup finely chopped onion

1   package (10 ounces) frozen mixed vegetables

1   tablespoon finely chopped parsley

2   teaspoons instant chicken bouillon granules

1/4   teaspoon dried marjoram leaves

1/8   teaspoon white pepper

1   cup half-and-half or milk, divided

1   cup water

2   tablespoons flour

    Cheese-flavored croutons

Put butter and onion into a 1-quart microwavable casserole. Cook uncovered at POWER HI for 2 to 3 minutes or until onion is tender. Add mixed vegetables, parsley, bouillon granules, marjoram, and pepper. Cook covered at POWER HI for 8 to 9 minutes or until vegetables are tender. Put vegetable mixture and 1/2 cup half-and-half into a blender or food processor; process until smooth. Return to casserole. Stir water into flour. Gradually stir water-flour mixture and remaining half-and-half into pureed mixture. Cook uncovered POWER HI for 3 minutes or until slightly thickened; stir once. Let stand 1 minute. Garnish with croutons.

4 servings

MINESTRONE GRATINÉE

½ pound lean ground beef

1 small onion, thinly sliced

1 can (16 ounces) whole tomatoes, drained, seeded, coarsely chopped

1 can (15½ ounces) Great Northern beans, drained

1 can (10½ ounces) condensed beef broth

1 cup water

½ cup frozen whole kernel corn

½ cup frozen cut green beans

½ cup cooked elbow macaroni

½ teaspoon dried marjoram leaves

¼ teaspoon dried oregano leaves

¼ teaspoon salt

⅛ teaspoon black pepper

1 bay leaf

4 slices French bread, ½-inch thick, toasted

2 slices (1-½ ounces) mozzarella cheese, cut in half

Put ground beef and onion in a 3-quart microwavable casserole. Cook uncovered at POWER HI for 2 minutes. Break up beef with a fork. Cook uncovered at POWER HI for 1½ to 2 minutes or until pink nearly disappears; drain. Add tomatoes, beans, broth, water, corn, green beans, macaroni, marjoram, oregano, salt, pepper, and bay leaf; mix well. Cook covered at POWER HI for 16 to 18 minutes or until vegetables are tender; stir once. Discard bay leaf. Ladle soup into four 15-ounce microwavable bowls; top with bread and mozzarella cheese. Place two bowls on turntable. Cook uncovered at POWER HI for 1 to 1-1/2 minutes or until cheese is melted.

Repeat with remaining bowls.

4 servings

ONION SOUP GRATINÉE

2 tablespoons butter or margarine

2 cups thinly sliced onions

1 tablespoon flour

1 can (14-½ ounces) beef broth

2 tablespoons white vermouth

2 teaspoons Dijon-style mustard

¼ teaspoon salt

⅛ teaspoon black pepper

2 slices stale French bread, 1-inch thick

½ cup shredded Swiss cheese

Put butter and onions into a 3-quart microwavable casserole. Cook covered at POWER HI for 6 to 7 minutes or until onions are tender. Add flour; mix well. Stir in broth, vermouth, mustard, salt, and pepper. Cook covered at POWER HI for 15 to 17 minutes or until slightly thickened, stir once. Remove casserole from oven. Preheat CONVECTION to 400°F. Place one slice of bread into each of two individual microwavable casseroles. Ladle hot soup over bread slice; top with Swiss cheese. Cook at CONVECTION (425°F) for 10 to 12 minutes or until cheese is lightly browned.

2 servings

CANADIAN SPLIT PEA SOUP

1   tablespoon butter or margarine

1   smoked ham hock (about 9 or 10 ounces)

1   cup finely chopped celery

1/2   cup finely chopped carrots

1/2   cup finely chopped onion

3   cups hot water

2   cans (14-1/2 ounces each) chicken broth

1   package (16 ounces) green split peas

1/2   teaspoon dried thyme leaves

1   bay leaf

1   teaspoon salt

1/4   teaspoon black pepper

   Dairy sour cream

Combine butter, ham hock, celery, carrots, and onion in a 4-quart microwavable casserole. Cook covered at POWER HI for 3 minutes. Stir in hot water, chicken broth, split peas, thyme, bay leaf, salt, and pepper. Cook covered at POWER HI for 10 minutes and then at POWER HI 5 for 70 to 80 minutes or until peas are tender; stir every 15 minutes. Let stand 10 minutes. Remove ham hock and cut off any meat; reserve meat. Discard bay leaf. Puree soup in a food processor or blender until smooth, if desired; return to casserole. Cook at POWER HI for 2 to 3 minutes or until thoroughly heated. Ladle soup into bowls, add reserved ham and garnish with a dollop of sour cream.

6 servings

MANHATTAN CLAM CHOWDER

1   tablespoon olive oil

1   medium potato, peeled, diced

3/4   cup finely chopped celery

1/2   cup finely chopped onion

2   cups bottled clam juice

1   can (16 ounces) whole tomatoes, drained, chopped

1   tablespoon chopped fresh parsley

1   bay leaf

1/4   teaspoon black pepper

1/8   teaspoon dried thyme leaves

1   can (10 ounces) whole baby clams, undrained

Combine olive oil, potato, celery, and onion in a 2-quart microwavable casserole. Cook uncovered at POWER HI for 4 to 5 minutes or until potatoes are just tender. Add clam juice, tomatoes, parsley, bay leaf, pepper, and thyme, mix well. Cook uncovered at POWER HI for 10 to 12 minutes to blend flavors; stir twice. Stir in clams. Cook uncovered at POWER HI for 2 to 2 1/2 minutes or until clams are hot. Let stand 1 minute. Discard bay leaf.

4 servings

Sandwiches

SLOPPY JOES

1   pound lean ground beef

1   cup finely chopped onions

2/3 cup ketchup

2   tablespoons pickle relish

1/2 teaspoon salt

1/4 teaspoon black pepper

6   hamburger buns, toasted

Put ground beef and onions into a 2-quart microwavable casserole. Cook uncovered at POWER HI for 2 minutes. Break up beef with a fork. Cook uncovered at POWER HI for 2 to 2 1/2 minutes or until pink nearly disappears; drain. Add ketchup, relish, salt, and pepper; mix well. Cook covered POWER HI for 3 to 4 minutes or until thoroughly heated; stir once. Let stand covered 5 minutes. Serve on buns.

6 servings

MEDITERRANEAN MARINADE

1/2 cup olive oil

2   tablespoons cider vinegar

1   small clove garlic, minced

1/4 teaspoon caraway seed

1/4 teaspoon cumin seed

1/4 teaspoon dried basil leaves

1/8 teaspoon black pepper

1/8 teaspoon dried oregano leaves

1   bay leaf

Combine olive oil, vinegar, garlic, caraway, cumin, basil, pepper, oregano, and bay leaf in a 2-cup glass measuring cup. Cook uncovered at POWER HI for 45 to 60 seconds or until hot. Discard bay leaf. Use while still warm.

2/3 cup

BARBECUED PORK SANDWICHES

2   pounds blade pork steaks

1   can (12 ounces) beer

1   small onion, thinly sliced

1   clove garlic, quartered

1   bay leaf

1/2 cup barbecue sauce

1/4 cup chili sauce

1/4 teaspoon black pepper

4   loaves (6 inch) pita bread (with pockets), cut in half crosswise

    Shredded lettuce or cole slaw

Put pork into a 3-quart microwavable casserole; add beer, onion, garlic, and bay leaf. Cook covered at POWER HI for 10 minutes; and then at POWER 3 for 50 to 55 minutes or until pork is tender. Let stand covered 10 minutes. Remove pork and onion; discard liquid. Let stand until cool enough to handle. Shred pork; return to casserole. Add reserved onion, barbecue sauce, chili sauce, and pepper; mix well. Cook covered at POWER HI for 3 to 4 minutes or until thoroughly heated. Serve in pita bread; top with shredded lettuce or cole slaw.

4 servings

BACON-CHEESEBURGERS

3   slices bacon

1   pound lean ground beef

2   teaspoons Worcestershire sauce

1/4 teaspoon onion powder

1/8 teaspoon black pepper

4   slices Swiss cheese

4   hamburger buns, toasted

Place bacon on a microwavable roast rack. Cover with double thickness of paper towel. Cook at POWER HI for 2 to 3 minutes or until just crisp. Cool; crumble. Combine bacon, ground beef, Worcestershire sauce, onion powder, and pepper in a mixing bowl. Shape mixture into four 1/2-inch thick patties; arrange on a microwavable and ovenproof roast rack. Place roast rack on Convection Rack. Place rack on turntable. Cook at COMBI HIGH for 10 to 12 minutes or until desired doneness. Top each patty with a Swiss cheese slice. Cook at COMBI HIGH for 45 to 60 seconds or until cheese is melted. Serve on buns.

4 servings

OPEN-FACE
ANTIPASTO MELTS

1   cup thinly sliced mushrooms

4   thin green pepper rings, cut in half

2   thin red onion slices, separated into rings

2   radishes, thinly sliced

1/4 cup Italian salad dressing

1   loaf (10 inches) French bread

1/4 cup mayonnaise

6   slices tomato

4   slices (1-1/2 ounces each) mozzarella or Swiss cheese

1/2 pound (8 ounces) sliced salami, bologna, turkey, roast beef, or ham

    Alfalfa sprouts

Combine mushrooms, green pepper, onion, and radishes in a small mixing bowl. Pour dressing over vegetables; toss lightly to coat. Set aside to marinate for 15 to 20 minutes. Preheat CONVECTION to 400°F. Slice bread loaf in half lengthwise, then in half crosswise to make four halves. Spread mayonnaise on each bread half; set aside. Drain vegetables; discard marinade. Layer each bread half with marinated vegetables, tomato, cheese, and meat. Place bread halves on Convection Rack. Place rack on turntable. Cook at CONVECTION (425°F) for 8 to 10 minutes or until cheese is melted. Garnish with alfalfa sprouts.

4 servings

OPEN-FACE
TUNA MELTS

1   can (6-1/2 ounces) tuna, drained and flaked

3/4 cup alfalfa sprouts

1/3 cup mayonnaise

1/3 cup sliced celery

1/4 cup thinly sliced green onions

1/2 teaspoon dried dill weed

1/8 teaspoon salt

    Dash black pepper

4   slices whole wheat bread, toasted

4   large slices tomato, cut 1/4-inch thick

4   slices American cheese

Preheat CONVECTION to 400°F. Combine tuna, alfalfa sprouts, mayonnaise, celery, green onions, dill weed, salt, and pepper; mix well. Place 1/4 of tuna mixture on each bread slice; spread evenly to edges. Top with tomato slice and then cheese slice. Place bread slices on Convection Rack. Place rack on turntable. Cook at CONVECTION (425°F) for 9 to 10 minutes or until cheese is melted.

4 servings

MEDITERRANEAN VEGETABLE SALAD IN PITA BREAD

Mediterranean Marinade (see recipe)

1/2 cup broccoli flowerets

1/2 cup cauliflower flowerets

1/2 cup sliced carrots

1/2 cup sliced celery

1 tablespoon olive oil

1/2 cup canned chick peas, rinsed and drained

1/2 cup quartered mushrooms

1/2 cup diced tomatoes

1/4 cup sliced green onions

4 loaves (6 inch) pita bread, with pockets

3/4 cup shredded Cheddar cheese

Prepare Mediterranean Marinade as directed in recipe; set aside to cool. Combine broccoli, cauliflower, carrots. celery, and olive oil in a 1-quart microwavable casserole. Cook covered at POWER HI for 4 to 5 minutes or until vegetables are just tender; drain excess liquid. Add chick peas, mushrooms, tomatoes, and green onions. Pour warm marinade over vegetables; stir gently to combine. Marinate covered in refrigerator for 1 to 2 hours to blend flavors; stir once. Cut pita loaves in half crosswise. Drain vegetables; discard marinade. Divide vegetable mixture evenly in all pita halves. Top each with Cheddar cheese. Stand each pita half cut side up in a 1 1/2 -quart microwavable baking dish. Cook uncovered at POWER HI for 3 to 4 minutes or until thoroughly heated and cheese is melted.

4 servings

DALLAS DOGGIES

8 slices bacon

4 hot dogs

2 slices Cheddar cheese, cut into 1/4-inch strips

4 hot dog buns, toasted

Arrange bacon between layers of paper towels on a microwavable roast rack. Cook at POWER HI for 3 1/2 to 4 minutes or until almost cooked. Cut a lengthwise pocket in each hot dog leaving 1/2 inch uncut at each end. Cut an X at each end to prevent curling. Stuff pocket with cheese strips. Wrap with two slices of partially cooked bacon. Secure with wooden picks. Arrange hot dogs in a circle on a paper towel-lined microwavable plate. Cover with paper towel. Cook at POWER HI for 2 to 2 1/2 minutes or until thoroughly heated and cheese is melted. Remove wooden picks. Serve on buns.

4 servings

Eggs and Pasta

SPINACH AND RICOTTA-STUFFED SHELLS

Mornay Sauce (see recipe)

1   package (10 ounces) frozen chopped spinach

2   tablespoons chopped fresh parsley

1   clove garlic, minced

1   tablespoon butter or margarine

1   package (3 ounces) cream cheese

1/2 cup finely chopped cooked ham

1/3 cup ricotta cheese

1   egg

1/4 teaspoon salt

1/8 teaspoon ground nutmeg

16   jumbo pasta shells, cooked and drained

Prepare Mornay Sauce as directed in recipe. Cover; set aside. Remove outer wrapping from spinach package. Place package on double thickness of paper towel. Cook at POWER HI for 5 to 6 minutes or until spinach is cooked. Let stand 2 minutes; set aside. Put parsley, garlic and butter into a 1 1/2 -quart microwavable casserole. Cook uncovered at POWER HI for 1 to 1 1/2 minutes or until butter is melted. Add cream cheese. Cook uncovered at POWER 5 for 30 to 60 seconds or until cream cheese is softened. Drain spinach thoroughly; add to cream cheese mixture. Add ham, ricotta cheese, egg, salt, and nutmeg; mix well. Stuff shells with spinach mixture. Pour prepared sauce into a 9-inch glass pie plate. Arrange shells in sauce. Cover with plastic wrap; vent. Cook covered at POWER 5 for 7 to 8 minutes or until spinach mixture is thoroughly heated. Serve on individual plates with sauce.

4 servings

MEXICAN STYLE EGGS

2 teaspoons olive oil

1/4 cup finely chopped onion

1 tablespoon finely chopped jalapeño pepper

1 clove garlic, minced

1 can (14-1/2 ounces) whole tomatoes, drained, chopped

1/4 teaspoon ground cumin

1/4 teaspoon salt

4 eggs

4 corn tortillas

1 tablespoon vegetable oil

Combine olive oil, onion, jalapeño pepper, and garlic in a 1-quart glass measuring cup. Cook uncovered at POWER HI for 1 to 2 minutes or until onions are tender-crisp. Add tomatoes, cumin, and salt; stir well. Cook uncovered at POWER HI for 4 to 5 minutes or until mixture boils; stir once. Cover with plastic wrap; set aside. Butter four 6-ounce custard cups and crack one egg into each. Pierce yolk with wooden pick. Cover with plastic wrap; vent. Arrange cups in a circle on turntable. Cook at POWER 5 for 3 to 3 1/2 minutes or until set. Let stand covered 2 minutes. Brush corn tortillas with vegetable oil. Arrange tortillas on a double thickness of paper towel on turntable. Cover with paper towel. Cook at POWER HI for 30 to 45 seconds or until thoroughly heated. Place one egg on one half of each tortilla. Fold tortilla over to cover egg; top with vegetable sauce. Serve immediately.

2 servings

CONFETTI MACARONI AND CHEESE

White Sauce (see recipe)

1 cup elbow macaroni (about 4 ounces), cooked, drained

1 cup boiled or baked ham, cut into 1/2-inch cubes

1 cup shredded Cheddar cheese

1/2 cup frozen peas

1/4 cup grated Parmesan cheese

1 tablespoon Dijon-style mustard

Prepare White Sauce as directed in recipe. Combine white sauce, macaroni, ham, Cheddar cheese, peas, Parmesan cheese, and mustard in a 2-quart microwavable casserole; mix thoroughly. Cook uncovered at POWER HI for 4 to 5 minutes or until hot; stir once. Let stand 1 minute.

4 servings

QUICHE DIJON

Pie Crust (see recipe)

6   slices bacon

1/4   cup diced green pepper

1/4   cup diced red pepper

1   tablespoon butter or margarine

4   eggs

1 1/2   cups half-and-half or milk

2   teaspoons Dijon-style mustard

1/4   teaspoon salt

1/8   teaspoon black pepper

1   cup grated Swiss cheese

Prepare Pie Crust and bake as directed in recipe; set aside. Place bacon on microwavable roast rack. Cover with double thickness of paper towel. Cook at POWER HI for 4 to 5 minutes or until crisp. Cool. Grumble; set aside. Put butter and green and red peppers into a 1-cup glass measuring cup. Cook uncovered at POWER HI for 2 to 3 minutes or until tender-crisp; set aside. Preheat CONVECTION to 325°F. Beat eggs, half-and-half, mustard, salt, and black pepper together in a medium mixing bowl. Layer bacon, peppers, and Swiss cheese evenly over baked pie crust. Pour egg mixture over cheese in crust. Cook at CONVECTION (325°F) for 35 to 40 minutes or until custard is set. Let stand 5 minutes.

8 servings

EGGS BENEDICT

Poached Eggs (see recipe)

Hollandaise Sauce (see recipe)

4   slices Canadian-style bacon

2   English muffins, split and toasted

Prepare Poached Eggs as directed in recipe. Let stand covered; set aside. Prepare Hollandaise Sauce as directed in recipe; set aside. Arrange bacon slices on a microwavable plate. Cover with plastic wrap; vent. Cook at POWER HI for 30 to 45 seconds or until thoroughly heated. Place one slice of bacon on each warm muffin half; top with poached egg and sauce. Serve immediately.

2 servings

POACHED EGGS

1 1/2   cups water

2   teaspoons white vinegar

4   eggs

Combine water and vinegar in a 2-quart microwavable casserole. Cook at POWER HI for 5 to 6 minutes or until water boils. Break each egg into a custard cup; pierce yolk with a wooden pick. Slip egg carefully into hot water. Cook covered at POWER 5 for 1 1/2 to 2 minutes or until whites are set and yolks are soft-set. Let stand covered for 1 minute. Remove from water with a slotted spoon.

2 servings

CALIFORNIA OMELETTE

½ cup chopped, seeded tomatoes

2 tablespoons sliced green onion

2 tablespoons sliced ripe olives or pimento-stuffed green olives

2 tablespoons butter or margarine, divided

⅛ teaspoon garlic powder

1 medium avocado, peeled, cut into 1-inch cubes

3 eggs, separated

1 tablespoon milk

¼ teaspoon salt

⅛ teaspoon black pepper

½ cup shredded Monterey Jack cheese, divided

Combine tomatoes, green onion, olives, 1 tablespoon butter, and garlic powder in a 1-quart microwavable casserole. Cook covered at POWER HI for 1 ½ to 2 minutes or until butter is melted. Add avocado; mix lightly. Set aside. Put remaining 1 tablespoon butter into a 10-inch glass pie plate. Cook at POWER HI for 30 to 45 seconds or until butter is melted; tilt pie plate to coat bottom. Set aside. In a medium mixing bowl, beat egg whites with an electric mixer at high speed until stiff but not dry. Beat egg yolks, milk, salt, and pepper in a small bowl. Fold egg yolk mixture into egg whites; pour into pie plate. Cook uncovered at POWER 5 for 5 to 6 minutes or until set. Spoon vegetable mixture over half of the omelette; sprinkle ¼ cup cheese over vegetables. Loosen omelette; sprinkle ¼ cup cheese over vegetables. Loosen omelette with spatula; gently fold in half. Sprinkle with remaining cheese. Cook uncovered at POWER 5 for 30 to 45 seconds or until cheese begins to melt. Let stand covered 1 minute.

2 servings

Chicken

CRISPY CHICKEN

1/4 cup milk

1/4 cup honey

2 1/2 to 3 pound chicken, cut into serving pieces

1 1/2 cups corn flake crumbs

1 teaspoon paprika

1/2 teaspoon salt

1/4 teaspoon coarsely ground black pepper

Combine milk and honey in a large mixing bowl; add chicken pieces. For coating, combine corn flake crumbs, paprika, salt, and pepper. Roll chicken pieces in coating mixture; coat evenly. Arrange chicken pieces on Convection Rack with thickest portions toward outside of rack. Place rack on turntable. Cook at COMBI HIGH for 25 to 30 minutes or until chicken is no longer pink and juices run clear. Let stand 5 minutes.

4 servings

CHICKEN CORDON BLEU

4 pieces skinless, boneless chicken breasts (about 4 ounces each)

2 ounces Swiss cheese, cut into thin strips

2 ounces baked ham, cut into thin strips

1 egg, lightly beaten

1/2 cup bread crumbs

Cut a lengthwise slit in center of thickest part of each chicken breast to form a pocket. Fill each pocket with 1/4 of the cheese and ham strips; secure with a wooden pick. Dip each filled breast into egg then roll in crumbs; coat evenly. Place breasts on a microwavable roast rack. Place roast rack on Convection Rack. Place rack on turntable. Cook at COMBI HIGH for 12 to 15 minutes or until chicken is thoroughly cooked. Remove wooden picks before serving.

4 servings

ROASTED CHICKEN WITH GARLIC AND ROOT VEGETABLES

2 carrots, pared, cut into 2-inch pieces

2 stalks celery, cut into 2-inch pieces

1 large sweet potato, pared, cut into 2-inch pieces

1 medium onion, peeled, cut into 2-inch pieces

1 small rutabaga, pared, cut into 2-inch pieces

2 tablespoons water

2 tablespoons butter or margarine, melted

5 cloves garlic, peeled, slivered

1/2 teaspoon dried rosemary leaves

1/4 teaspoon dried thyme leaves

2 1/2 to 3 pound whole chicken

Fresh thyme

Put carrots, celery, sweet potato, onion, rutabaga, and water into a 3-quart microwavable casserole. Cook covered at POWER HI for 10 minutes or until fork-tender; stir once. Set aside. Meanwhile, place garlic, rosemary, and thyme into cavity of chicken. Place chicken on microwavable roast rack; brush with butter. Place Convection Rake on turntable. Cook at COMBI HIGH for 30 to 35 minutes or until chicken is no longer pink and juices run clear; brush with butter halfway through cooking. Temperature in thigh should reach 180°F and temperature in breast should reach 170°F when done. Remove chicken and place in center of microwavable and ovenproof platter; surround with vegetables. Drizzle vegetables with chicken juices, if desired. Cook at COMBI HIGH for 5 to 7 minutes or until vegetables are thoroughly heated. Garnish with fresh thyme, if desired.

4 servings

CHICKEN POT PIE

White Sauce (see recipe)

1 tablespoon butter or margarine

1/2 cup thinly sliced carrots

1/2 cup thinly sliced celery

1/2 cup thinly sliced mushrooms

1/2 cup snow pea pods (about 2 inches each)

1/4 cup diced red pepper

2 cups cubed, cooked chicken

1 refrigerated, ready-to-bake pie crust

Prepare White Sauce as directed in recipe; set aside. Put butter, carrots, celery, mushrooms, pea pods, and red pepper into a 1-quart microwavable and ovenproof casserole. Cook covered at POWER HI for 4 to 5 minutes or until vegetables are tender crisp; stir once. Preheat CONVECTION to 375°F. Add chicken and white sauce to vegetables; stir well. Top with crust; trim and flute edge. Cut steam vent in center of crust. Cook at CONVECTION (375°F) for 14 to 16 minutes or until sauce is hot and crust is lightly browned.

4 servings

HOISIN CHICKEN WITH WALNUTS AND RED PEPPER

2 tablespoons soy sauce

1 tablespoon dry sherry

1 tablespoon vegetable oil

1 clove garlic, minced

$\frac{1}{4}$ teaspoon dried red pepper flakes

12 ounces skinless, boneless chicken breasts, cut into 2 × $\frac{3}{4}$-inch strips

6 green onions, cut into 1-inch lengths

1 medium red pepper, thinly sliced

$\frac{1}{2}$ cup walnut halves

$\frac{1}{3}$ cup Hoisin sauce

Hot cooked rice

Green onion brush

Combine soy sauce, sherry, oil, garlic, and red pepper flakes in a small mixing bowl; stir in chicken to coat. Refrigerate covered 30 minutes. Combine chicken strips, marinade, green onions, red pepper, and walnuts in a 1$\frac{1}{2}$-quart microwavable casserole. Cook covered at POWER HI for 6 to 7 minutes or until chicken is no longer pink; stir once. Drain; stir in Hoisin sauce. Let stand covered 1 to 2 minutes. Serve over rice. Garnish with green onion brush.

4 servings

CHICKEN CACCIATORE

2$\frac{1}{2}$ to 3 pound chicken, cut into serving pieces, skinned

1 medium green pepper, cut into thin strips

1 medium onion, thinly sliced

2 tablespoons olive oil

1$\frac{1}{2}$ teaspoons Italian seasoning

$\frac{1}{2}$ teaspoon salt

$\frac{1}{4}$ teaspoon black pepper

1 bay leaf

$\frac{1}{2}$ cup dry white wine

1 can (16 ounces) whole tomatoes, drained, coarsely chopped

1 can (15 ounces) tomato sauce

1 cup sliced fresh mushrooms (about 4 ounces)

Hot cooked spaghetti

Put chicken pieces, green pepper, onion, olive oil, Italian seasoning, salt, pepper, bay leaf, and wine into a 3-quart microwavable casserole. Cook covered at POWER HI for 10 minutes; turn over and rearrange chicken halfway through cooking. Add tomatoes, tomato sauce, and mushrooms; stir to combine. Cook covered at POWER HI for 10 to 12 minutes or until chicken is tender and flavors are blended. Let stand 5 minutes. Discard bay leaf. Serve over hot cooked spaghetti.

4 servings

CHICKEN ENCHILADAS

1 cup finely chopped green pepper

½ cup finely chopped zucchini

1 clove garlic, minced

1 can (10 ounces) enchilada sauce

1 can (8 ounces) tomato sauce

2 cups chopped, cooked chicken

½ cup refried beans

½ teaspoon dried oregano leaves

¼ teaspoon ground cumin

¼ teaspoon salt

8 (6-½ inch) flour tortillas

1 cup shredded Cheddar cheese

Combine green pepper, zucchini, and garlic in a 1½-quart microwavable casserole. Cook covered at POWER HI for 3 to 4 minutes or until vegetables are tender. Combine enchilada and tomato sauces; reserve ½ cup. Add remaining sauce to green pepper mixture. Stir in chicken, refried beans, oregano, cumin, and salt; mix well. Cook covered at POWER HI for 3 to 4 minutes or until thoroughly heated; stir once. Set aside. Soften tortillas by placing between damp paper towels. Cook at POWER HI for 45 to 60 seconds or until warm. Spoon ½ cup of chicken mixture into center of each tortilla; roll up. Place seam side down in a 1½-quart microwavable baking dish. Pour reserved sauce over tortillas. Cook uncovered at POWER HI for 6 to 7 minutes or until thoroughly heated. Sprinkle with Cheddar cheese. Cook uncovered at POWER HI for 1 to 2 minutes or until cheese is melted. Let stand 2 minutes.

4 servings

CHICKEN MILANO

1 egg, beaten

1 teaspoon water

⅔ cup corn flake crumbs

2 tablespoons grated Parmesan cheese

2 tablespoons grated Romano cheese

1 teaspoon dried basil leaves

1 teaspoon salt

½ teaspoon dried oregano leaves

1 clove garlic, minced

1 tablespoon chopped fresh parsley

¾ teaspoon paprika

¼ teaspoon black pepper

2½ to 3 pound chicken, cut into serving pieces

Beat egg and water in a shallow bowl. For coating, combine crumbs, Parmesan and Romano cheeses, basil, salt, oregano, garlic, parsley, paprika, and pepper on a sheet of waxed paper. Dip chicken pieces into egg mixture then roll in coating mixture. Arrange chicken pieces on Convection Rack with thickest portions toward outside of rack. Place rack on turntable. Cook at COMBI HIGH for 25 to 30 minutes or until chicken is no longer pink and juices run clear. Let stand 5 minutes.

4 servings

CORNISH GAME HENS WITH INDONESIEN RICE STUFFING

1/2 cup coarsely chopped apples

1/4 cup coarsely chopped celery

1 tablespoon thinly sliced green onion

1 cup cooked brown rice

2 tablespoons raisins

2 tablespoons coarsely chopped pecans

1/8 teaspoon ground cardamon

1/8 teaspoon ground nutmeg

1/8 teaspoon sage

1/4 teaspoon salt

2 Cornish game hens (1 to 1 1/2 pounds each)

Glaze:

1/2 cup fresh orange juice

2 tablespoons honey

2 tablespoons Dijon-style mustard

1 tablespoon orange marmalade

1 tablespoon cornstarch

Orange juice

Combine apples, celery, and green onion in a 1-quart microwavable casserole. Cook covered at POWER HI for 2 to 3 minutes or until apples are tender. Stir in rice, raisins, pecans, cardamon, nutmeg, sage, and salt. Spoon stuffing into cavities of hens. Place hens breast side up on microwavable and ovenproof roast rack. Place Convection Rack on turntable. Place roast rack on Convection Rack. To make glaze, combine orange juice, honey, mustard, and marmalade in a 2-cup glass measuring cup. Pour 1/3 cup of glaze over hens. Cook at COMBI HIGH for 35 to 40 minutes or until hens are no longer pink and juices run clear; brush with glaze.

Temperature in breast should reach 170°F when done. Let stand 5 minutes tented with foil to keep warm. Add enough orange juice to remaining glaze to make 1 cup; stir in cornstarch. Cook uncovered at POWER HI for 2 to 2 1/2 minutes or until slightly thickened; stir once. Serve with warm Cornish game hens.

2 servings

SPANISH CHICKEN

2 1/2 to 3 pound chicken, cut into serving pieces

1 can (14 ounces) artichoke hearts, drained, cut into halves

3 small white onions, cut into quarters

1/3 cup small ripe olives

1/3 cup pimento-stuffed green olives

1 can (10-3/4 ounces) condensed chicken broth

1/4 cup dry white wine

1 tablespoon fresh lemon juice

1/2 teaspoon dried sage leaves, crushed

1/4 teaspoon whole allspice

1/4 teaspoon whole black peppercorns

Arrange chicken pieces in a 3-quart microwavable casserole with thickest portions to outside. Top with artichoke hearts, onions, and olives. Combine broth, wine, lemon juice, sage, allspice, and peppercorns in a 2-cup glass measuring cup; stir well. Pour mixture over chicken. Cook covered at POWER HI for 18 to 20 minutes or until chicken is no longer pink and juices run clear; stir sauce twice. Let stand covered 5 minutes.

4 servings

Fish

BAKED STUFFED SHRIMP

3   tablespoons butter or margarine

1   clove garlic, minced

1   cup fresh bread crumbs

2   tablespoons chopped fresh parsley

2   tablespoons finely diced red pepper

1/4   teaspoon salt

1/8   teaspoon black pepper

1   pound uncooked shrimp, shelled, deveined, tails left on

Put butter and garlic into a 2-cup glass measuring cup. Cook uncovered at POWER HI for 1 minutes. Add bread crumbs, parsley, red pepper, salt, and pepper; mix well. To butterfly shrimp slice lengthwise almost through the back without separating; spread open. Preheat CONVECTION to 400°F. Arrange shrimp cut side down in a 10-inch glass pie plate with tails towards the center. Divide crumb mixture evenly on top of each shrimp. Cook at CONVECTION (425°F) for 13 to 15 minutes or until shrimp are opaque and crumbs are lightly browned. Serve immediately.

4 servings

FILLET OF SOLE WITH WHITE MUSHROOM SAUCE

   White Sauce (see recipe)

1 1/2   cups thinly sliced fresh mushrooms

1/4   cup thinly sliced green onions

4   sole fillets (about 1 pound)

2   tablespoons white vermouth

1/2   teaspoon salt

Prepare White Sauce in a 1-quart glass measuring cup; set aside. Butter an 8×8×2-inch glass baking dish. Cover bottom of dish with mushrooms and green onions. Roll fillets and secure with wooden picks. Place fillets on sliced vegetables; sprinkle with vermouth and then salt. Cover with plastic wrap; vent. Cook covered at POWER HI for 4 to 5 minutes or until fish is opaque. Let stand covered 2 minutes. Remove wooden picks from fillets. Put fillets onto serving platter; cover with foil to keep warm. Drain vegetables; discard cooking liquid. Stir vegetables into white sauce. Cook uncovered at POWER HI for 2 to 2 1/2 minutes or until thoroughly heated. Spoon sauce over fillets; serve immediately.

4 servings

FLOUNDER WITH FRESH VEGETABLES

1   cup thinly sliced mushrooms

3/4   cup coarsely chopped, seeded, peeled fresh plum tomatoes (about 4 ounces)

1/4   cup coarsely chopped green pepper

1/4   cup coarsely chopped red pepper

1/4   cup thinly sliced green onions

1   clove garlic, minced

3   tablespoons chopped fresh parsley

1   pound flounder fillets

1/4   teaspoon salt

1/8   teaspoon black pepper

1/8   teaspoon dried dill weed

1/8   teaspoon dried thyme leaves

1   tablespoon dry white wine

1   tablespoon fresh lemon juice

Combine mushrooms, tomatoes, green and red peppers, green onions, and garlic in a 1-quart glass measuring cup. Cover with plastic wrap; vent. Cook at POWER HI for 3 to 4 minutes or until vegetables are tender-crisp. Add parsley; mix well. Set aside. Arrange flounder fillets with thickest portions toward outside edge in an 8×8×2-inch glass baking dish. Sprinkle with salt, pepper, dill weed, and thyme. Spoon vegetable mixture over fish; sprinkle with wine and lemon juice. Cover with plastic wrap; vent. Cook at POWER HI for 5 to 6 minutes or until fish is opaque and flakes easily when tested with a fork. Let stand covered 2 minutes.

4 servings

SHRIMP PRIMAVERA

White Sauce (see recipe)

2   tablespoons butter or margarine

1   small zucchini (about 6 ounces), cut lenghwise into quarters sliced 1/2-inch thick

1   cup broccoli flowerets

1   cup quartered fresh mushrooms

1   cup (2-inch lengths) asparagus

1/2   cup thinly sliced carrots

2   tablespoons butter

1/2   pound medium shrimp, shelled, deveined

2   tablespoons chopped fresh basil leaves

4   ounces fettucine noodles, cooked, drained

1/4   cup grated Parmesan cheese

Prepare thin White Sauce as directed in recipe; set aside. Put butter, zucchini, broccoli, mushrooms, asparagus, and carrots into 2-quart microwavable casserole. Cook covered at POWER HI for 5 to 6 minutes or until vegetables are tender; drain. Stir in shrimp. Cook covered at POWER HI for 1 minute. Add basil and reserved white sauce; stir to coat shrimp mixture. Cook uncovered at POWER HI for 2½ to 3 minutes or until shrimp are opaque. Let stand 1 minute. Pour vegetable-shrimp mixture over cooked noodles; sprinkle with Parmesan cheese. Serve immediately.

4 servings

BAKED SALMON FILLETS WITH CUCUMBER SAUCE

1½ cups chopped, pared cucumber

2 tablespoons thinly sliced green onion

2 tablespoons chopped fresh mint leaves

½ teaspoon salt, divided

¼ teaspoon white pepper, divided

½ cup dairy sour cream

¼ cup plain yogurt

¼ teaspoon paprika

2 salmon fillets (7 to 8 ounces each), skinned

1 tablespoon butter or margarine

1 tablespoon lime juice

   Fresh chives

   Mint leaves

For cucumber sauce, combine cucumber, green onion, mint leaves, ¼ teaspoon salt, and ⅛ teaspoon pepper in a small bowl. Let stand 15 minutes. Add sour cream, yogurt, and paprika; mix well.

Cover and refrigerate. Put salmon fillets into an 8×8×2-inch glass baking dish.

Dot with butter; sprinkle with lime juice and remaining salt and pepper. Place Convection Rack on turntable. Place baking dish on rack. Cook uncovered at COMBI LOW for 15 to 20 minutes or until fish flakes easily when tested with fork. Garnish with fresh chives and mint leaves. Serve with sauce. May also be served chilled.

2 servings

MINI CRAB SOUFFLÉS

2 tablespoons butter or margarine

¼ cup thinly sliced green onions

2 tablespoons flour

⅓ cup white vermouth

1 cup heavy cream

1 can (6 ounces) crabmeat, drained and flaked

½ cup fresh bread crumbs

1 egg, separated

½ teaspoon salt

⅛ teaspoon black pepper

Put butter and green onions into a l-quart glass measuring cup. Cook uncovered at POWER HI for 1 minute, stir in flour. Gradually pour vermouth and then cream into butter-flour mixture stirring constantly with a wire whisk. Cook uncovered at POWER HI for 4 to 5 minutes or until thickened; stir twice with whisk. Add crabmeat, bread crumbs, egg yolk, salt, and pepper; mix well. Beat egg white in a small mixing bowl at high speed with an electric mixer until soft peaks form. Fold egg white into crab mixture. Spoon mixture into four 6-ounce custard cups. Cook uncovered at COMBI LOW for 21 to 23 minutes or until set. Serve immediately.

4 servings

RED SNAPPER WITH JULIENNE OF GARDEN VEGETABLES

2   tablespoons butter or margarine

1   cup julienned carrots

1   cup julienned celery

1   cup julienned leeks

1   cup julienned red pepper

1   pound red snapper fillets, cut into 4 serving pieces

1/4 cup white vermouth

1/2 teaspoon salt

1/4 teaspoon black pepper

1/2 cup heavy cream

2   tablespoons brandy

Combine butter, carrots, celery, leeks, and red pepper in a 2-quart microwavable casserole. Cook covered at POWER HI for 7 to 8 minutes or until vegetables are tender. Set aside. Arrange fillets skin side down in a 1 1/2 -quart microwavable glass baking dish; sprinkle with vermouth, salt, and black pepper. Cover with plastic wrap; vent. Cook at POWER HI for 4 to 5 minutes or until fish is opaque and flakes easily when tested with a fork. Remove fish and place on a serving platter; reserve cooking liquid in baking dish. Spoon cooked vegetables with a slotted spoon over fish; pour cooking liquid from casserole into baking dish. Cover fish and vegetables to keep warm. Stir cream and brandy into combined cooking liquids. Cook uncovered at POWER HI for 3 to 4 minutes or until thoroughly heated. Pour sauce over fish and vegetable. Serve immediately.

4 servings

HALIBUT STEAKS WITH TOMATO-HERB SAUCE

1   tablespoon butter or margarine

1/4 cup finely chopped onion

1   clove garlic, minced

2   cups chopped, seeded tomatoes

2   tablespoons dry white wine

2   tablespoons chopped fresh parsley

2   tablespoons chopped fresh basil leaves

4   small halibut steaks, (about 1 pound), cut 1-inch thick

2   tablespoons lemon juice

1/4 teaspoon salt

1/8 teaspoon black pepper

Put butter, onion, and garlic into a 1 1/2 -quart baking dish. Cook uncovered at POWER HI for 2 to 3 minutes or until vegetables are tender-crisp. Add tomatoes, wine, parsley, and basil; stir well. Cook uncovered at POWER HI for 3 to 4 minutes or until thoroughly heated. Place halibut steaks on top of tomato-herb sauce. Sprinkle fish with lemon juice, salt, and pepper. Cover with plastic wrap; vent. Cook covered at POWER HI for 6 to 7 minutes or until fish is opaque and flakes easily with a fork. Let stand covered for 2 minutes before serving.

4 servings

JAMBALAYA

½ pound Italian sausage

1 tablespoon olive oil

½ cup coarsely chopped celery

½ cup coarsely chopped green pepper

½ cup coarsely chopped onion

1 pound bone-in chicken breasts, cut into serving size pieces

1 can (16 ounces) whole tomatoes, drained, seeded, coarsely chopped

1 can (10 ¾ ounces) condensed chicken broth

1 cup uncooked long-grain white rice

¼ cup tomato paste

1 clove garlic, minced

1 bay leaf

¼ teaspoon ground red pepper
  pound medium shrimp, shelled, deveined
  Sliced green onion

Pierce sausage and put on a microwavable plate. Cover with plastic wrap; vent. Cook covered at POWER HI for 4 to 5 minutes or until sausage is no longer pink. Let stand 10 minutes. Cut into 1-inch pieces; set aside. Combine olive oil, celery, green pepper, and onion in a 3-quart microwavable casserole. Cook uncovered at POWER HI for 5 minutes; stir once. Add sausage, chicken pieces, tomatoes, chicken broth, rice, tomato paste, garlic, bay leaf, and red pepper; stir well. Cook covered at POWER HI for 25 to 27 minutes or until rice is tender; stir twice. Stir in shrimp. Cook covered at POWER HI for 3 to 4 minutes or until shrimp are opaque. Discard bay leaf. Garnish with sliced green onion.

6 to 8 servings

SCALLOPS PROVENÇAL

4 tablespoons olive oil, divided

¼ cup thinly sliced mushrooms

1 clove garlic, minced

2 medium tomatoes, peeled, seeded, coarsely chopped

2 tablespoons dry white wine

2 tablespoons chopped fresh basil leaves

2 tablespoons chopped fresh parsley

½ teaspoon salt

¼ teaspoon black pepper

1 pound sea scallops
  Hot cooked rice or pasta

Combine 3 tablespoons olive oil, mushrooms, and garlic in a 1-quart microwavable casserole. Cook uncovered at POWER HI for 2 minutes. Add tomatoes, wine, basil, parsley, salt, and pepper; mix well. Cook uncovered at POWER HI for 2 minutes. Set sauce aside. Combine remaining olive oil and scallops in a 1½ -quart microwavable baking dish. Cover with plastic wrap; vent. Cook at POWER HI for 5 to 6 minutes or until scallops are opaque; stir once. Drain. Add scallops to reserved tomato sauce; stir well. Cook uncovered at POWER HI for 1 to 1½ minutes or until thoroughly heated. Serve over cooked rice or pasta.

4 servings

Beef

BEEF AND VEGETABLES IN CABERNET SAUCE

1½ pounds boneless beef chuck top blade pot roast, cut into 1-inch cubes

¼ cup flour

1 cup sliced carrots (about ½-inch thick)

1 cup sliced celery (about ½-inch thick)

1 cup diced onions

1 cup quartered fresh mushrooms

1 cup cubed, pared potatoes

1 can (16 ounces) tomatoes, drained, coarsely chopped

1½ cups beef broth

1 cup Cabernet wine

1 bay leaf

⅛ teaspoon dried thyme leaves

¼ teaspoon black pepper

Put beef and flour into a large plastic food storage bag; shake to coat beef evenly. Empty beef mixture into a 3-quart microwavable casserole. Add carrots, celery, onions, mushrooms, potatoes, tomatoes, beef broth, wine, bay leaf, thyme, and pepper. Cook covered at POWER HI for 10 minutes; stir. Cook covered at POWER 5 for 60 to 70 minutes or until meat is tender; stir three times. Discard bay leaf.

6 to 8 servings

HOMESTYLE MEAT LOAF

½ cup finely chopped onion

¼ cup finely chopped celery

1 tablespoon butter

1 clove garlic, minced

1½ pounds lean ground beef

1 slice white bread, crust trimmed, torn into small pieces

1 egg, slightly beaten

2 teaspoons Worcestershire sauce

¼ teaspoon salt

⅛ teaspoon black pepper

¼ cup ketchup

Put onion, celery, butter, and garlic into a 2-cup glass measuring cup. Cook uncovered at POWER HI for 3 minutes; set aside. Put beef into a medium mixing bowl. Add cooked vegetables, bread, egg, Worcestershire sauce, salt, and pepper; mix well. Shape beef mixture into a rectangular loaf, about 6×4-inches; place on a microwavable and ovenproof roast rack. Spread ketchup on top. Place Convection Rack on turntable. Place roast rack on Convection Rack. Cook at COMBI HIGH for 30 to 35 minutes or until internal temperature reaches 165°F. Let stand 5 minutes.

6 servings

GARLIC BEEF WITH CARROTS

1 tablespoon dry white wine

1 tablespoon soy sauce

1 teaspoon sugar

½ teaspoon salt

¼ teaspoon sesame oil

⅛ teaspoon ground ginger

1 pound boneless beef sirloin steak, cut into
⅛-inch strips

½ cup thinly sliced green onions, divided

½ cup thinly sliced green pepper strips

3 medium carrots, diagonally sliced

2 tablespoons vegetable oil

2 cloves garlic, minced

2 teaspoons cornstarch

2 teaspoons cold water

Hot cooked rice

Combine wine, soy sauce, sugar, salt, sesame oil, and ginger in a medium mixing bowl. Add beef, ¼ cup green onions, and green pepper; stir to coat. Refrigerate covered for 30 minutes. Put carrots into a 1-quart microwavable casserole. Cook covered at POWER HI for 2 to 3 minutes or until tender-crisp; set aside. Cook oil and garlic in a 2-quart microwavable casserole at POWER HI for 1 minute. Stir in meat mixture. Cook uncovered at POWER HI for 3 minutes; stir once. Stir in reserved carrots; set aside. Mix cornstarch and water in a small bowl. Stir into meat-vegetable mixture. Cook uncovered at POWER HI for 6 to 7 minutes or until beef is no longer pink and sauce thickens; stir once. Let stand 2 minutes. Serve with hot cooked rice. Garnish with remaining green onions.

4 servings

BEEF GOULASH

1 to 1 ½ pounds boneless beef chuck top
blade pot roast, cut into ¾-inch cubes

¼ cup flour

1 can (16 ounces) whole tomatoes, drained,
chopped

2 medium potatoes, pared, cut into 8 pieces
each

1 cup thinly sliced carrots

½ cup coarsely chopped onions

⅔ cup water

1 tablespoon lemon juice

1½ teaspoons instant beef bouillon granules

1½ teaspoons paprika

½ teaspoon garlic powder

¼ teaspoon dried dill weed

Put beef and flour into a large plastic food storage bag; shake to coat beef. Empty beef-flour mixture into a 3-quart microwavable casserole. Stir in tomatoes, potoates, carrots, onions, water, lemon juice, bouillon, paprika, garlic, and dill weed. Cook covered at POWER HI for 5 minutes and then at POWER 5 for 65 to 70 minutes or until beef is tender; stir three or four times. Let stand covered 10 minutes.

4 to 6 servings

CHILI AND BEANS WITH CORNBREAD TOPPING

2 tablespoons olive oil

1½ pounds beef chuck T-bone steak, cut into ¼-inch cubes

1 cup coarsely chopped onions

2 cloves garlic, minced

1 tablespoon chili powder

½ teaspoon salt

½ teaspoon dried marjoram leaves

¼ teaspoon dried oregano leaves

½ teaspoon ground cumin

¼ teaspoon coriander seed

1 small bay leaf

1 can (15 ounces) tomato sauce

1 can (15- ½ ounces) red kidney beans, rinsed, drained

Indian Cornbread (see recipe)

Combine olive oil, beef cubes, onions, and garlic in a 3-quart microwavable casserole. Add chili powder, salt, marjoram, oregano, cumin, coriander seed, and bay leaf; mix well. Cook covered at POWER HI for 7 to 8 minutes or until beef is no longer pink; stir once. Stir in tomato sauce and kidney beans. Cook covered at POWER 7 for 10 minutes; stir once. Let stand 10 minutes. Discard bay leaf. Prepare cornbread as directed in recipe; drop spoonfuls around edge of chili. Cook at COMBI HIGH for 14 to 16 minutes or until cornbread is golden brown.

8 servings

LEMON-GARLIC BEEF BROCHETTES

¼ cup olive oil

2 tablespoons lemon juice

1 clove garlic, minced

1 teaspoon black pepper

1 pound boneless beef sirloin steak (about 1-inch thick), cut into 1-inch cubes

3 small red potatoes, unpared, cut into quarters

1 tablespoon water

1 jar (6 ounces) marinated artichoke hearts, drained

8 pitted extra large ripe olives

Combine olive oil, lemon juice, garlic, and pepper in a mixing bowl. Add beef; stir to coat. Marinate covered in refrigerator for 1 hour. Drain beef; reserve marinade. Put potatoes and water into a 1-quart microwavable casserole. Cook covered at POWER HI for 5 to 6 minutes or until tender; set aside. Preheat CONVECTION to 400°F. On 10-inch wooden skewers, alternate beef with artichoke and olive then three potato quarters; continue to alternate beef with artichoke and olive, ending with beef. Arrange skewers on Convection Rack. Brush with reserved marinade. Place rack on turntable. Cook at CONVECTION (425°F) for 16 to 20 minutes or until beef is cooked to desired doneness.

4 servings

ZUCCHINI-WRAPPED MEATBALLS

4 small zucchini (about 1 pound)

1 pound lean ground beef

1 cup cooked long-grained white rice

2 tablespoons finely chopped onion

1 egg, beaten

1/2 teaspoon salt

1/8 teaspoon black pepper

1/8 teaspoon ground allspice

1/8 teaspoon garlic powder

1 can (16 ounces) whole tomatoes, drained, chopped

1 can (8 ounces) tomato sauce

1/2 teaspoon dried rosemary leaves

   Hot cooked rice

Cut zucchini lengthwise into sixteen $1/4$ -inch thick slices; set aside. For meatballs, combine ground beef, rice, onion, egg, salt, pepper, allspice, and garlic powder in a medium mixing bowl; mix thoroughly. Shape into 16 meatballs. Wrap a zucchini strip around each meatball; secure with a wooden pick. Place in an 8×8×2-inch glass baking dish. Cook uncovered at POWER HI for 8 to 9 minutes or until beef is no longer pink. Drain; rearrange meatballs. For sauce, combine tomatoes, tomato sauce, and rosemary in a small mixing bowl. Pour sauce over meatballs. Cover with plastic wrap; vent. Cook at POWER HI for 3 to 4 minutes or until zucchini is tender and sauce is thoroughly heated. Let stand 1 minute. Remove picks before eating. Serve over rice.

4 servings

BEEF STROGANOFF

2 tablespoons butter or margarine

1 1/2 cups sliced fresh mushrooms (about 6 ounces)

1 small onion, thinly sliced, separated into rings

1 1/2 pounds boneless beef round steak, trimmed

1 can (10 3/4 ounces) condensed cream of mushroom soup

1/4 cup water

1 tablespoon chopped fresh parsley or 1/2 teaspoon dried parsley

1/2 teaspoon dry mustard

1/4 teaspoon dried sage leaves, crushed

1/8 teaspoon black pepper

1/3 cup dairy sour cream

Put butter, mushrooms, and onion into a 2-quart microwavable casserole. Cook uncovered at POWER HI for 2 1/2 to 3 minutes or until vegetables are tender. Slice beef diagonally across the grain into 4× 1/4 -inch strips. Add beef strips to vegetable mixture; mix well. Cook uncovered at POWER HI 4 to 4 1/2 minutes or until pink nearly disappers. Combine soup, water, parsley, dry mustard, sage, and pepper in a 2-cup glass measuring cup; stir into beef mixture. Cook covered at POWER HI for 5 to 6 minutes; stir once. Stir in sour cream. Let stand covered 5 minutes.

4 servings

Pork

PORK BACK RIBS WITH BARBECUE SAUCE

1½ pounds pork loin back ribs

½ cup water

1 cup barbecue sauce

Cut ribs into serving size pieces. Place ribs bone side down in a large cooking bag. Place bag in an 8×8×2-inch glass baking dish; add water. Close bag loosely with microwavable closure. Cook at POWER HI for 5 minutes and then at POWER 5 for 35 to 45 minutes or until meat is fork-tender; turn ribs over halfway through cooking. Remove ribs from cooking bag; place on microwavable and ovenproof roast rack. Brush with barbecue sauce. Place Convection Rack on turntable. Place roast rack on Convection Rack. Cook at COMBI LOW for 5 minutes. Turn ribs over; brush with barbecue sauce. Cook at COMBI LOW for 5 minutes.

2 servings

ROASTED PORK LOIN

2 tablespoons olive oil

1 clove garlic, minced

1 teaspoon dried oregano leaves

½ teaspoon black pepper, coarsely ground

¼ cup Dijon style mustard

1½ pound boneless pork loin blade roast, rolled and tied

Combine olive oil, garlic, oregano, and pepper in a large food storage bag. Roll meat in seasoned oil mixture to coat. Refrigerate for 30 minutes; turn once. Place Convection Rack on turntable.

Place meat on microwavable and ovenproof roast rack. Spread mustard over top and sides of meat. Place roast rack on Convection Rack. Cook at COMBI LOW for 40 to 45 minutes or until internal temperature reaches 170°F. Cover with foil. Let stand covered 10 minutes. Serve thinly sliced.

6 servings

APRICOT-STUFFED PORK CHOPS

4   boneless, butterflied pork loin chops, (about 2 pounds, 1-inch thick)

¼   cup butter or margarine, melted

¼   cup finely chopped dried figs

1   can (8-¾ ounces) apricot halves, drained and finely chopped (reserve ¼ cup syrup)

1   package (6 ounces) herb-seasoned stuffing mix

¾   cup chicken broth

½   teaspoon dried marjoram leaves

¼   teaspoon black pepper

Make two pockets in each pork chop, cutting from outside edge almost to center. For stuffing, combine butter, figs, apricots, stuffing mix, chicken broth, reserved syrup, marjoram, and pepper in a mixing bowl; mix well. Fill pockets with stuffing mixture. Arrange chops on microwavable and ovenproof roast rack with thickest portions towards outside. Place Convection Rack on turntable. Place roast rack on Convection Rack. Cook at COMBI LOW for 35 to 40 minutes or until internal temperature reaches 170°F and juices run clear. Cut chops in half through uncut center portion to serve.

8 servings

GLAZED HAM

3½ to 4 pound fully cooked boneless ham

Cranberry-Raisin Glaze:

1   can (16 ounces) whole cranberry sauce

½   cup raisins

½   cup packed brown sugar

½   teaspoon cinnamon

2   tablespoons bourbon

2 cups

(OR)

Orange-Walnut Glaze:

1   jar (10 ounces) orange marmalade

¼   cup finely chopped walnuts

2   tablespoons sliced green onion

1   tablespoon dark corn syrup

1   tablespoon white cider vinegar

1   teaspoon dry mustard

1 ½ cups

Score diamond shapes into top of ham. Place ham scored side down on microwavable roast rack; set aside. For desired glaze, combine all ingredients in a 1-quart glass measuring cup. Cook uncovered at POWER HI for 2 to 3 minutes or until thoroughly heated; stir once. Set aside. Cover ham with waxed paper. Cook covered at POWER 5 for 30 minutes. Turn ham over; brush with glaze. Cover with waxed paper. Cook at POWER 5 for 20 to 25 minutes or until internal temperature reaches 120°F; brush twice with glaze during cooking. Cover with foil. Let stand 10 minutes before slicing. Serve with remaining glaze.

14 to 16 servings

PORK ROAST WITH HERBS

3   cloves garlic, minced, divided

1½ teaspoons dried rosemary leaves. divided

1   teaspoon grated fresh lemon peel

¼   teaspoon crushed dried sage leaves

¼   teaspoon black pepper, divided

3   pound rolled pork loin roast, boneless

2   tablespoons fresh lemon juice

⅓   cup unseasoned dry bread crumbs

1   tablespoon chopped fresh parsley

½   teaspoon dried thyme leaves

½   teaspoon dried oregano leaves

    Lemon and carrot slices

    Fresh herbs

Combine 2 cloves garlic, 1 teaspoon rosemary, lemon peel, sage, and ⅛ teaspoon black pepper in a small bowl. Untie roast and rub inside surface with herb mixture. Roll and tie roast with string. Brush lemon juice on outside surface. Combine bread crumbs, parsley, thyme, oregano, and remaining garlic, rosemary, and pepper on a sheet of waxed paper. Roll roast in crumb mixture; press onto roast. Place roast fat side down on Convection Rack. Cook at COMBI LOW for 60 to 65 minutes or until meat thermometer inserted in center of meat registers 170°F; turn over halfway through cooking. Let stand tented with foil 10 minutes before slicing. Garnish with lemon and carrot slices and fresh herbs.

12 servings

MEDITERRANEAN STEW

2   tablespoons butter or margarine

1   small eggplant, pared, cut into ¾-inch cubes

½   cup sliced celery

½   cup coarsely chopped onion

2   pounds pork stew meat, cut into ¾-inch cubes

1   can (16 ounces) whole tomatoes, chopped

1   can (6 ounces) tomato paste

12 pitted ripe olives

12 pimiento-stuffed olives

1½ teaspoons Italian seasoning

1   teaspoon instant chicken bouillon granules

½   teaspoon salt

⅛   teaspoon black pepper

    Hot cooked rice

Put butter, eggplant, celery, and onion into a 3-quart microwavable casserole. Cook covered at POWER HI for 4 minutes. Stir in pork, tomatoes, tomato paste, olives, Italian seasoning, bouillon, salt, and pepper. Cook covered at POWER HI for 10 minutes and then at POWER 5 for 45 to 50 minutes or until pork is tender; stir twice. Let stand covered 10 minutes before serving. Serve over hot cooked rice.

8 servings

WINE AND HERB BRAISED RIBS

3 pounds pork spareribs, cut into 2-rib pieces

1 medium onion, thinly sliced

2 bay leaves

2/3 cup tomato juice

3/4 cup dry white wine, divided

1/2 teaspoon dried parsley leaves

1/2 teaspoon dried tarragon leaves

2 slices bacon, finely chopped

1/4 cup finely chopped carrot

1/4 cup finely chopped onion

1 clove garlic, minced

2 tablespoons flour

1/4 teaspoon black pepper

2 tablespoons tomato paste

1/2 cup beef broth

1/2 cup barbecue sauce

Put ribs, onion slices, and bay leaves into a large oven cooking bag. Place in an 8×8×2-inch glass baking dish; set aside. Combine tomato juice, 1/2 cup wine, parsley, and tarragon in a small bowl; pour mixture into bag. Close bag loosely with microwavable closure. Cook at POWER 5 for 60 to 70 minutes or until pork is tender. Turn ribs over and rearrange halfway through cooking.

Do not overlap ribs in bag. Set aside. Combine bacon, carrot, onion, and garlic in a 2-quart microwavable casserole. Cook covered at POWER HI for 6 1/2 to 7 1/2 minutes or until vegetables are tender and bacon is crisp; stir once. Add flour, pepper, and tomato paste; mix well. Stir in beef broth, barbecue sauce, and remaining wine. Cook uncovered at POWER HI for until thickened; stir once. Remove ribs from cooking bag. Arrange on microwavable roast rack; brush with sauce and cook uncovered at POWER HI for 6½ to 7½ minutes or until hot. Serve with remaining sauce.

4 servings

Vegetables
and Side Orders

LEMON CREAMED SPINACH

White Sauce (see recipe)

1 package (10 ounces) frozen chopped spinach

1 teaspoon freshly grated lemon peel

1/4 teaspoon salt

Prepare White Sauce as directed in recipe; set aside. Remove outer wrapping from spinach package. Place package on double thickness of paper towels on turntable. Cook at POWER HI for 5 to 6 minutes or until spinach is cooked. Let stand 2 minutes. Drain spinach thoroughly. Combine spinach, lemon peel, reserved white sauce, and salt in a 1-quart microwavable casserole. Cook uncovered at POWER 7 for 4 to 5 minutes or until thoroughly heated. Let stand 2 minutes.

4 servings

CORN AND PEPPER RELISH

2 tablespoons vegetable oil

1/3 cup chopped celery

1/3 cup diced green pepper

1/3 cup diced red pepper

1/4 cup chopped onion

1/4 cup cider vinegar

2 tablespoons sugar

2 cans (12 ounces each) whole kernel corn, drained

Combine oil, celery, green and red pepper, and onion in a 1 1/2 -quart microwavable casserole. Cook uncovered at POWER HI for 1 1/2 to 2 minutes or until vegetables are tender-crisp. Stir in cider vinegar and sugar. Cook at POWER HI for 1 1/2 to 2 minutes or until heated through. Add corn; mix well. Chill before serving.

4 cups

SPICY BLACK BEANS

2 tablespoons olive oil

1/2 cup diced red pepper

1/2 cup diced onion

1 clove garlic, minced

2 cans (16 ounces each) black beans, rinsed, drained

1 can (15 ounces) tomato sauce

1 teaspoon minced jalapeño pepper

1/2 teaspoon ground cumin

1/2 teaspoon salt

1/4 teaspoon ground coriander

1 package (8 ounces) refrigerated crescent dinner rolls

Combine olive oil, red pepper, onion, and garlic in an 8-inch round glass cake dish. Cook uncovered at POWER HI for 2 1/2 to 3 minutes or until vegetables are tender-crisp; stir once. Add beans, tomato sauce, jalapeño pepper, cumin, salt, and coriander; mix well. Cover with plastic wrap; vent. Cook at POWER 7 for 6 minutes; set aside. Unroll and separate dough into eight triangles. Arrange triangles on a generously floured surface with points toward the center to form a 9 1/2-inch circle. Fold points back to form a 2-inch circle in the center. Press edges together to seal; transfer to top of bean mixture. Press to seal around edge of dish. Cook at COMBI HIGH for 15 to 17 minutes or until golden brown.

6 to 8 servings

BROCCOLI WITH HOLLANDAISE SAUCE

1 1/2 pounds broccoli, cut into 4-inch spears

1 tablespoon water

3 egg yolks

1 tablespoon fresh lemon juice

1/8 teaspoon white pepper

1/2 cup butter or margarine

Pimento strips

Lemon wedges

Arrange broccoli spears in a 1 1/2-quart microwavable baking dish with flowerets towards center of dish; add water. Cover with plastic wrap; vent. Cook covered at POWER HI for 8 to 10 minutes or until broccoli is tender; drain. Cover to keep warm; set aside. Blend egg yolks, lemon juice, and pepper with a wire whisk in a 1-quart microwavable casserole; set aside. Put butter into a 2-cup glass measuring cup. Cook uncovered at POWER HI for 1 to 1 1/2 minutes or until butter is melted. Gradually pour butter into egg mixture stirring constantly with whisk. Cook uncovered at POWER 5 for 1 to 1 1/2 minutes or until thickened; stir three times with whisk. Serve over reserved broccoli. Garnish with pimento strips and lemon wedges.

4 servings

FRESH VEGETABLE KABOBS

½   cup butter or margarine

1   tablespoon lemon juice

1   teaspoon seasoned salt

½   teaspoon dried dill weed (or ½ teaspoon
    fresh chopped)

1   small bunch broccoli (about 1 pound), cut
    into 2-inch spears

1   medium zucchini (about ½ pound), cut into
    1-inch wedges

1   large red pepper, cut into 1½-inch squares

3   small onions, cut into quarters

12 medium fresh mushrooms

1   small cauliflower (about 2 pounds), cut into
    2-inch pieces

Put butter into a 2-cup glass measuring cup. Cook uncovered at POWER HI for 1 to 1¼ minutes or until butter is melted. Stir in lemon juice, seasoned salt, and dill weed. To assemble kabobs, alternate broccoli, zucchini, red pepper, onion, mushroom, and cauliflower on twelve 8-inch wooden skewers. Arrange kabobs on a 10-inch round microwavable plate; brush with butter sauce. Cover with plastic wrap; vent. Cook covered at POWER HI for 4 to 5 minutes or until vegetables are tender. Let stand covered 1 to 2 minutes. Repeat with remaining kabobs. Remove cover and brush with additional butter sauce before serving.

6 servings

VEGETABLE CUSTARDS

1   tablespoon butter or margarine

¼   cup finely chopped onion

½   cup finely chopped broccoli

½   cup finely grated carrot

¼   teaspoon salt

⅛   teaspoon white pepper

1½ cups milk

3   eggs, beaten

Put butter and onion into a 1-quart microwavable casserole. Cook uncovered at POWER HI for 3 minutes. Add broccoli, carrot, salt, and pepper; stir well. Cook uncovered at POWER HI for 3½ to 4 minutes or until vegetables are tender. Pour milk into a 1-quart glass measuring cup. Cook uncovered at POWER HI for 3 to 4 minutes or until very hot but not boiling. Stir in cooked vegetables and eggs. Pour mixture into four 6-ounce glass custard cups. Arrange in a circle on turntable. Cook uncovered at POWER 5 for 9 to 11 minutes or until custard is fully set and knife inserted near center comes out clean. Let stand for 5 minutes before serving.

4 servings

HOT AND SAVORY POTATO SALAD

4 medium baking potatoes (about 2 pounds), scrubbed

2 tablespoons vegetable oil

4 slices bacon, diced

1/2 cup coarsely chopped onion

1/2 cup coarsely chopped celery

1/4 cup cider vinegar

1 tablespoon sugar

1 tablespoon Dijon-style mustard

1/2 teaspoon salt

1/8 teaspoon ground red pepper

1 tablespoon chopped fresh parsley

Pierce potatoes several times with a fork. Place on double thickness of paper towel on turntable. Cook at POWER HI for 10 to 12 minutes or until soft to the touch; turn over halfway through cooking. Allow to cool for 1 hour. Peel potatoes; cut into 1/2-inch thick slices; set aside. Combine oil, bacon, onion, and celery in a 2-quart microwavable casserole. Cook uncovered at POWER HI for 5 to 6 minutes or until vegetables are tender-crisp; stir once. Add potatoes, vinegar, sugar, mustard, salt, and red pepper; stir gently to coat. Cook covered at POWER HI for 2 to 3 minutes or until thoroughly heated; stir once. Let stand for 1 minute. Add chopped parsley; stir gently. Serve immediately.

4 servings

CORNBREAD AND SAUSAGE DRESSING

1/4 pound fresh pork sausage

2 cups stale crumbled cornbread

1/2 cup finely chopped celery

1/2 cup finely chopped onion

1 tablespoon chopped fresh parsley

1 egg, lightly beaten

1 cup chicken broth

1/4 teaspoon salt

1/4 teaspoon black pepper

Crumble sausage into a 1-quart microwavable casserole. Cook uncovered at POWER HI for 2 to 2 1/2 minutes or until sausage is no longer pink; stir once to break pork apart. Add cornbread, celery, onion, parsley, and egg to sausage; mix well. Add broth, salt, and pepper; mix lightly. Cook covered at POWER HI for 6 to 7 minutes or until thoroughly heated. Let stand 2 minutes. Stir before serving.

4 servings

BAKED STUFFED TOMATOES

4   large, ripe tomatoes

1/2   pound lean ground beef

1   tablespoon olive oil

1/4   cup chopped onion

1/2   cup uncooked long-grain white rice

3/4   cup chicken broth

1/2   cup smoked gouda cheese, cut into 1/4-inch cubes

1   tablespoon chopped fresh parsley

1/2   teaspoon salt

1/8   teaspoon coarsely ground black pepper

Cut off top quarter of each tomato; set aside. Scoop out tomato pulp leaving 1/4 inch thick shell. Discard seeds; chop remaining pulp. Set aside. Put ground beef into a 1-quart microwavable casserole. Cook uncovered at POWER HI for 2 to 3 minutes or until pink nearly disappears; stir once to break up beef. Drain; set aside. Combine olive oil and onion in a 1-quart microwavable casserole. Cook uncovered at POWER HI for 2 to 3 minutes or until onion is tender. Add rice, reserved tomato pulp, and chicken broth mixture to onions. Cook covered at POWER HI for 17 to 18 minutes or until rice is tender. Add reserved ground beef, cheese, parsley, salt, and pepper; mix well. Spoon rice mixture into tomatoes; place reserved tomato quarters on top. Place tomatoes in an 8×8×2-inch glass baking dish. Cook uncovered at POWER HI for 3 to 4 minutes or until thoroughly heated and tomatoes are tender. Let stand 1 minute.

4 servings

HERB ROASTED POTATOES

1   pound new potatoes, scrubbed

1/4   cup vegetable oil

1   tablespoon chopped fresh parsley

1/2   teaspoon paprika

1/2   teaspoon salt

1/4   teaspoon coarsely ground black pepper

1/4   teaspoon dried rosemary leaves

1/8   teaspoon dried thyme leaves

Cut potatoes into quarters. Combine potatoes, oil, parsley, paprika, salt, pepper, rosemary, and thyme in a medium mixing bowl; toss lightly to coat. Turn potato mixture into an 8×8×2-inch glass baking dish. Cook uncovered at COMBI HIGH for 18 to 23 minutes or until potatoes are tender and lightly browned; stir twice. Let stand 3 to 4 minutes before serving.

4 servings

PROSCIUTTO AND WALNUT STUFFED ONIONS

2   medium Spanish onions (about 12 ounces each), peeled

¼   cup plus 3 tablespoons water, divided

2   thin slices prosciutto ham (about 1 ounce), cut into ½-inch squares

½   cup dry bread crumbs

¼   cup coarsely chopped walnuts

1   tablespoon chopped fresh parsley

1   clove garlic, minced

¼   teaspoon salt

⅛   teaspoon black pepper

2   tablespoons butter or margarine, melted

Cut onions in half crosswise; cut a thin slice from the root end to allow onions to stand upright. Arrange onions in a 8×8×2-inch glass baking dish; add ¼ cup water. Cover with plastic wrap; vent. Cook at POWER HI for 5 to 6 minutes or until onion pierces easily with tip of sharp knife. Let stand covered 5 minutes; drain. When cool enough to handle, remove center core from onions leaving ½-inch shell. Chop enough of the onion cores to make ¼ cup; reserve remaining onion for other uses. Combine ¼ cup onion, ham, bread crumbs, walnuts, parsley, garlic, salt, and pepper in a medium bowl; mix well. Fill each onion shell with ¼ of stuffing mixture. Return to baking dish; drizzle with butter. Place Convection Rack on turntable. Place dish on rack. Cook uncovered at COMBI HIGH for 12 to 15 minutes or until thoroughly heated.

4 servings

RATATOUILLE

3   tablespoons olive oil

3   cloves garlic, minced

1   cup thinly sliced onions

1   medium green pepper, thinly sliced

1   medium eggplant, peeled, cut into ½-inch cubes

2   medium zucchini, sliced ¼-inch thick

4   plum tomatoes, seeded, coarsely chopped

1   can (8 ounces) tomato sauce

1   bay leaf

1   tablespoon chopped fresh parsley

½   teaspoon salt

½   teaspoon coarsely ground black pepper

Combine olive oil, garlic, onion, and green pepper in a 3-quart microwavable casserole. Cook uncovered at POWER HI for 3 to 4 minutes or until vegetables are tender-crisp. Add eggplant and zucchini; stir to coat. Cook uncovered at POWER HI for 5 minutes; stir once. Add tomatoes, tomato sauce, bay leaf, parsley, salt, and pepper, mix well. Cook covered at POWER HI for 10 to 11 minutes or until vegetables are tender; stir once. Let stand 5 minutes. Discard bay leaf. Stir before serving.

6 servings

ORANGE-MAPLE ACORN SQUASH

1/4 cup maple syrup

1/4 cup orange juice

2 tablespoons packed brown sugar

2 tablespoons honey

1 tablespoon butter or margarine

1 tablespoon lemon juice

1 teaspoon grated fresh orange peel

1/4 teaspoon grated fresh lemon peel

1/8 teaspoon cinnamon

2 medium acorn squash (about 3 pounds)

For glaze, combine maple syrup, orange juice, brown sugar, honey, butter, lemon juice, orange peel, lemon peel, and cinnamon in a 2-cup glass measuring cup. Cook uncovered at POWER HI for 6 to 7 minutes; set aside. Wash and place squash on double thickness of paper towel on turntable. Cook at POWER HI for 5 minutes. Carefully cut each squash into quarters; remove seeds and fibers. Arrange quarters on a 10-inch glass pie plate; spoon glaze into squash quarters. Cover with plastic wrap; vent. Cook at POWER HI for 14 to 15 minutes or until squash is tender. Baste with glaze halfway through cooking. Let stand 5 mintues.

8 servings

GLAZED CARROTS

1 pound carrots, cut into 1/4-inch diagonal slices

1/4 cup chicken broth

1 tablespoon sugar

1 tablespoon butter or margarine

Combine carrots, broth, sugar, and butter in a 1 1/2 quart microwavable casserole. Cook covered at POWER HI for 8 to 9 minutes or until carrots are tender; stir once. Let stand covered 2 minutes.

4 servings

WILTED SPINACH SALAD

1/4 cup olive oil

1 tablespoon fresh lemon juice

1/2 teaspoon black pepper

1/2 teaspoon ground nutmeg

1/2 teaspoon salt

1 pound spinach, washed, stems removed

Combine olive oil, lemon juice, pepper, nutmeg, and salt in a 3-quart microwavable casserole. Cook uncovered at POWER HI for 3 to 4 minutes or until hot. Add spinach; toss to coat with oil mixture. Cook uncovered at POWER HI for 1 minute. Stir well., Let stand covered 2 to 3 minutes.

4 servings

TWICE BAKED POTATOES

4   medium baking potatoes (about 2 pounds), scrubbed

2   slices bacon

1/2 cup shredded Cheddar cheese

1/2 cup dairy sour cream

1/4 cup half-and-half or milk

1   egg, beaten

2   tablespoons butter or margarine

2   tablespoons chopped fresh parsley

1   tablespoon thinly sliced green onions

1/4 teaspoon salt

1/8 teaspoon white pepper

Pierce potatoes several times with a fork. Place on a double thickness of paper towel on turntable. Cook at POWER HI for 11 to 13 minutes or until potatoes are tender; turn over halfway through cooking. Set aside. Place bacon on microwavable roast rack; cover with paper towel. Cook at POWER HI for 1 1/2 to 2 1/2 minutes or until just crisp. Cool and crumble; set aside. Cut a thin slice about 1/4-inch from top of each potato. Scoop out centers to within 1/4-inch of edge. Reserve shells. Preheat CONVECTION to 350°F. Combine potato plup, crumbled bacon, Cheddar cheese, sour cream, half-and-half, egg, butter, parsley, green onion, salt, and pepper in a large mixing bowl. Beat at medium speed of electric mixer until blended. Spoon 1/4 of the potato mixture into each shell. Arrange potatoes in a 1 1/2-quart baking dish. Cook at CONVECTION (350°F) for 25 to 30 minutes or until lightly browned and thoroughly heated.

4 servings

BACON SCALLOPED POTATOES

2   slices bacon

2   large baking potatoes (about 1 3/4 pounds), peeled and thinly sliced

1/2 teaspoon salt

1/4 teaspoon white pepper

1   cup half-and-half or milk

1   cup shredded Cheddar cheese

1   tablespoon butter or margarine

Place bacon on microwavable roast rack; cover with paper towel. Cook at POWER HI for 1 1/2 to 2 1/2 minutes or until just crisp. Cool; crumble. Layer potatoes and bacon in an 8×8×2-inch glass baking dish; sprinkle with salt and pepper. Pour half-and-half over potatoes. Sprinkle Cheddar cheese over potatoes; dot with butter. Cook uncovered at COMBI HIGH for 20 to 25 minutes or until potatoes are tender.

4 servings

COUNTRY BUTTERMILK BISCUITS

2   cups flour

1   tablespoon baking powder

1   tablespoon sugar

$1/2$ teaspoon baking soda

$1/2$ teaspoon salt

$1/2$ cup butter or margarine, cut into small pieces

$2/3$ cup buttermilk

Preheat CONVECTION to 400°F. Combine flour, baking powder, sugar, baking soda, and salt in a medium mixing bowl. Cut butter into flour until mixture resembles coarse crumbs; add buttermilk. Mix just until dry ingredients are moistened; do not overmix. Turn dough out onto a lightly floured surface; knead 8 to 10 times. Roll or pat out 1/2-inch thick. Cut with 2-inch cutter dipped in flour. Place cut biscuits directly on ungreased turntable. Cook CONVECTION (425°F) for 10 to 12 minutes or until lightly browned. Serve warm.

20 biscuits

INDIAN CORNBREAD

$1^{1/4}$ cups yellow corn meal

$3/4$ cup flour

2   tablespoons sugar

2   tablespoons baking powder

$1/2$ teaspoon salt

2   eggs

$2/3$ cup milk

2   tablespoons vegetable oil

Preheat CONVECTION to 400°F. Combine corn meal, flour, sugar, baking powder, and salt in a mixing bowl. Add eggs, milk, and oil; combine until dry ingredients are just moistened. Pour into a greased 8-inch square baking pan. Cook at CONVECTION (425°F) for 12 to 15 minutes or until a wooden pick inserted near center comes out clean.

8 servings

TOASTED GARLIC BREAD

$1/2$ cup butter or margarine, softened

3   tablespoons chopped fresh parsley

2   cloves garlic, minced

$1/4$ teaspoon salt

$1/4$ teaspoon black pepper

1   loaf (10-inch) round Italian bread

2   tablespoon grated Parmesan cheese

Preheat CONVECTION to 400°F. Combine butter, parsley, garlic, salt, and pepper in a small mixing bowl; mix well. Cut bread loaf in half lengthwise; spread seasoned butter on each half.

Sprinkle with Parmesan cheese. Place Convection Rack on turntable. Place one bread half on rack. Cook at CONVECTION (425°F) for 5 to 7 minutes or until lightly browned. Repeat with remaining bread half.

8 servings

Sauces

HOLLANDIAISE SAUCE

3   egg yolks

1   tablespoon fresh lemon juice

1/8   teaspoon white pepper

1/2   cup butter

Blend egg yolks, lemon juice, and pepper with a wire whisk in a 1-quart microwavable casserole; set aside. Put butter into a 2-cup glass measuring cup. Cook uncovered at POWER HI for 1 to 1½ minutes or until butter is melted. Gradually pour butter into egg mixture stirring constantly with whisk. Cook uncovered at POWER 5 for 1 to 1½ minutes or until thickened; stir three times with whisk. Serve immediately.

Serve with cooked fresh vegetables or eggs.

3/4 cup

MORNAY SAUCE

1   tablespoon butter or margarine

1   tablespoon flour

1/8   teaspoon ground nutmeg

1½   cups half-and-half or milk

1/3   cup grated Parmesan cheese

Put butter into a 1-quart glass measuring cup. Cook uncovered at POWER HI for 30 to 45 seconds or until butter is melted. Stir in flour and nutmeg making a smooth paste. Gradually add half-and-half; stir well. Cook uncovered at POWER HI for 2 to 3 minutes or until thickened; stir twice. Stir in Parmesan cheese. Let stand 1 minute. Serve as sauce for stuffed pasta shells.

About 1 3/4 cups

WHITE SAUCE

1   tablespoon butter or margarine

1   tablespoon flour

1/4   teaspoon salt

1/8   teaspoon pepper

1   cup half-and-half or milk

Put butter into a 2-cup glass measuring cup. Cook uncovered at POWER HI for 30 to 60 seconds or until butter is melted. Stir in flour, salt, and pepper making a smooth paste. Gradually add milk; stir well. Cook uncovered at POWER HI for 2 to 3 minutes or until thickened; stir vigorously two or three times. Let stand 1 minute.

Serve as a light sauce for entrées or open-faced sandwiches.

1 cup

VARIATIONS

Medium White Sauce: Increase butter and flour to 2 tablespoons.

Continue as directed. Serve with cooked vegetables for a creamed side dish.

Thick White Sauce: Increase butter and flour to 3 tablespoons.

Continue as directed. Serve as topping for entrées of chicken or turkey or in casseroles.

BUTTERSCOTCH SAUCE

1/3   cup packed brown sugar

1/4   cup sugar

4   teaspoons flour

1/4   cup butter or margarine, softened

1/4   cup half-and-half

1   tablespoon light corn syrup

1/4   teaspoon vanilla extract

    Dash salt

Combine brown sugar, sugar, and flour in a 1-quart glass measuring cup. Add butter, half-and-half, corn syrup, vanilla, and salt; mix well. Cook uncovered at POWER HI for 1 1/2 to 2 minutes or until mixture boils; stir well. Cook uncovered at POWER 7 for 4 to 5 minutes or until mixture thickens; stir twice. Serve warm over ice cream or cake.

About 2/3 cup

RED MEAT SAUCE

1/2   pound lean ground beef

1/2   pound bulk Italian sausage

1   cup coarsely chopped onions

3/4   cup coarsely chopped green pepper

1   clove garlic, minced

1   can (28 ounces) whole tomatoes, drained, chopped

1   can (8 ounces) tomato sauce

1   can (6 ounces) tomato paste

1 1/2   cups sliced fresh mushrooms (about 6 ounces)

2   tablespoons olive oil

2   teaspoons Italian seasoning

2   teaspoons sugar

1/8   teaspoon ground cloves

1   bay leaf

Crumble ground beef and sausage into a 3-quart microwavable casserole. Add onions, green pepper, and garlic. Cook uncovered at POWER HI for 5 1/2 to 6 minutes or until meat is no longer pink; stir once to break meat apart. Drain. Add tomatoes, tomato sauce and paste, mushrooms, olive oil, Italian seasoning, sugar, cloves, and bay leaf; mix well. Cook uncovered at POWER HI for 20 to 25 minutes or until vegetables are tender; stir three times. Discard bay leaf. Serve with pasta.

About 4 1/2 cups

BARBECUE SAUCE

1   teaspoon vegetable oil

1   cup finely chopped onion

2   cloves garlic, minced

1   can (8 ounces) tomato sauce

1/2   cup ketchup

1/4   cup packed brown sugar

1/4   cup cider vinegar

1   tablespoon Dijon-style mustard

1   tablespoon fresh lemon juice

1   tablespoon Worcestershire sauce

1   teaspoon horseradish

1/2   teaspoon ground ginger

Combine oil, onion, and garlic, in a 1-quart glass measuring cup. Cook uncovered at POWER HI for 3 minutes; stir once. Stir in tomato sauce, ketchup, brown sugar, vinegar, mustard, lemon juice, Worcestershire sauce, horseradish, and ginger. Cover with plastic wrap; vent. Cook covered at POWER HI for 4 to 5 minutes or until boiling; stir once. Cook covered at POWER 5 for 10 minutes to blend flavors. Let stand 3 minutes. Serve with pork spareribs or chicken.

2 2/3 cups

Desserts

PIE CRUST

1 cup flour

1/4 teaspoon salt

6 tablespoons vegetable shortening

3 to 4 tablespoons water

Combine flour and salt in a mixing bowl. Cut shortening into flour to form coarse crumbs. Sprinkle with water 1 tablespoon at a time; mix with a fork until particles are moistened and cling together. Form dough into a ball. Preheat CONVECTION to 400°F Place dough on a lightly floured surface. Roll out 1/8-inch thick (about a 12-inch circle) and place in a 9-inch glass pie plate. Trim and flute edge. Prick sides and bottom of crust with a fork. Cook at CONVECTION (425°F) for 10 to 12 minutes or until dry and opaque.

One 9-inch crust

GRAHAM CRACKER CRUST

1/4 cup butter or margarine

11/4 cups graham cracker crumbs

2 tablespoons sugar

1/4 teaspoon cinnamon

Put butter in a 9-inch glass pie plate. Cook uncovered at POWER HI for 1 to 1 1/4 minutes or until butter is melted. Mix crumbs, sugar, and cinnamon; add to butter. Mix well. Press mixture firmly against bottom and sides of pie plate. Cook uncovered at POWER HI for 1 1/2 to 2 minutes or until set. Cool completely before filling.

One 9-inch crust

CHOCOLATE FONDUE

1   package (12 ounces) semi-sweet chocolate
     pieces
1/2 cup heavy cream
1/3 cup coffee-flavored liqueur
     Assorted fresh fruit (strawberries, oranges,
     kiwifruit, or pineapple), cut-up

Combine chocolate pieces and cream in a
1-quart glass measuring cup. Cook uncovered at POWER 7 for 3 to 4 minutes or
until chocolate pieces are completely melted;
stir twice. Stir in liqueur. Pour into serving
bowl. Dip assorted fruits into fondue using
fondue forks or skewers. May also be served as a sauce for ice cream.

About 2 cups

CITRUS DELIGHT

2   extra large grapefruit (about 1½ pounds
     each)
1/4 cup chopped walnuts
2   tablespoons raisins
2   tablespoons packed brown sugar
1/4 teaspoon cinnamon

Cut grapefruits in half crosswise. Loosen
each section with a knife. Combine walnuts,
raisins, brown sugar, and cinnamon in a mixing bowl. Spread 2 tablespoons of mixture
on each grapefruit half. Place directly on
turntable. Cook uncovered at POWER HI for
6 to 8 minutes or until thoroughly heated. Let
stand 2 minutes.

4 servings

CREAM CHEESE AND RICOTTA FRUIT PIE

     Graham Cracker Crust (see recipe)
2   packages (3 ounces each) cream cheese
2/3 cup ricotta cheese
5   tablespoons sugar, divided
2   eggs
1   tablespoon fresh lemon juice
1/3 cup sour cream
1   cup sliced fresh strawberries, peaches, or
     grapes

Prepare Graham Cracker Crust as directed
in recipe; set aside. Put cream cheese into
a 2-quart microwavable casserole. Cook uncovered at POWER 5 for 1 to 1 ½ minutes
or until softened. Add ricotta cheese, 4 tablespoons sugar, eggs, and lemon juice. Beat
at medium speed with electric mixer until
smooth. Pour into prepared graham cracker
crust. Cook uncovered at POWER 5 for 11
to 13 minutes or until edges of filling are firm
and center is almost set. Let stand on counter
for 10 minutes. Combine sour cream and remaining 1 tablespoon sugar in a small mixing bowl. Spread on top of pie. Refrigerate
at least 2 hours. Top with fresh fruit before
serving.

One-9-inch pie

APPLE-PEAR CRISP

6 cups pared, thinly sliced apples (about 6 medium)

2 cups pared, thinly sliced pears (about 2 medium)

2 tablespoons sugar

1 tablespoon fresh lime juice

1/2 teaspoon grated fresh lime peel

1/2 teaspoon ground ginger, divided

1/8 teaspoon ground allspice

1/2 cup flour

1/3 cup packed brown sugar

1/3 cup chopped almonds

1/4 cup quick oats, uncooked

1/8 teaspoon salt

5 tablespoons butter or maragine, cut into small pieces

Combine apples, pears, sugar, lime juice, lime peel, 1/4 teaspoon ginger, and allspice in an 8×8×2-inch glass baking dish; mix well. Combine flour, brown sugar, almonds, oats, remaining ginger, salt, and butter in a small mixing bowl. Cut butter into flour mixture with a pastry blender to form coarse crumbs. Sprinkle crumb mixture evenly over fruit. Cook at COMBI HIGH for 18 to 20 minutes or until fruit is tender and topping is crisp. Let stand 5 minutes.

8 servings

APPLESAUCE CAKE

2 cups flour

1 teaspoon baking soda

1 teaspoon cinnamon

1/2 teaspoon ground nutmeg

1/4 teaspoon ground cloves

1/4 teaspoon salt

1/2 cup butter or margarine, softened

1 cup sugar

2 eggs

3/4 cup applesauce

1/2 cup raisins

1/2 cup coarsely chopped walnuts

Preheat CONVECTION to 350°F. Sift together flour, baking soda, cinnamon, nutmeg, cloves, and salt; set aside. In a medium mixing bowl cream butter and sugar with electric mixer at medium speed until light. Add eggs, one at a time; beat well after each addition for a total of 2 minutes. Stir in flour mixture alternately with applesauce; mix until blended after each addition. Fold in raisins and walnuts. Pour mixture into a greased 10-cup fluted tube pan. Cook at CONVECTION (350°F) for 40 to 45 minutes or until wooden pick inserted near center comes out clean. Cool 15 minutes; remove from pan.

1 tube cake

NEW ORLEANS BREAD PUDDING

3 cups (1-inch cubes) stale French or Italian bread

½ cup chopped pecans

½ cup raisins

3 eggs

2 cups milk

⅔ cup sugar

2 tablespoons butter or margarine, melted

1 teaspoon vanilla extract

½ teaspoon cinnamon

¼ teaspoon ground nutmeg

Combine bread cubes, pecans, and raisins in an 8-inch square baking pan. Combine eggs, milk, sugar, butter, vanilla, cinnamon, and nutmeg; mix well. Pour egg-milk mixture over bread cubes. Allow mixture to stand 20 minutes. Preheat CONVECTION to 350°F. Cook CONVECTION (350°F) for 30 to 35 minutes or until custard is set and knife inserted near center comes out clean.

8 servings

PECAN PIE

Pie Crust (see recipe)

4 eggs

1 cup dark corn syrup

½ cup sugar

2 tablespoons butter or margarine, melted

1 tablespoon vanilla extract

¼ teaspoon salt

2 cups pecan halves

Prepare Pie Crust and bake as directed in recipe; set aside. Preheat CONVECTION to 375°F. Combine eggs, corn syrup, sugar, butter, vanilla, and salt in a 1-quart glass measuring cup. Beat with electric mixer 1 minute or until well blended. Add pecans; mix well. Pour mixture into baked pie crust. Cook at CONVECTION (375°F) for 35 to 40 minutes or until set. Allow to cool before serving.

One 9-inch pie

GLAZED BANANAS

½ cup packed brown sugar

1 tablespoon fresh lemon juice

1 tablespoon butter or margarine

2 bananas, peeled, cut lengthwise into halves

Combine brown sugar, lemon juice, and butter in a 2-cup glass measuring cup Cook uncovered at POWER HI for 1 to 1½ minutes or until sugar is dissolved; stir once. Arrange bananas cut side up in a 8×8×2-inch glass baking dish. Pour sauce over bananas. Cook uncovered at POWER HI for 2 minutes. Turn over and rearrange; spoon sauce over top. Cook uncovered at POWER HI for 1 to 2 minutes or until bananas are hot. Let stand 1 minute. Serve immediately.

4 servings

CINNAMON CRESCENTS

1/4 cup raisins

3 tablespoons coarsely chopped pecans

2 tablespoons sugar

2 tablespoons cinnamon

1 package (8 ounces) refrigerated crescent dinner rolls

2 tablespoons butter or margarine, melted

Preheat CONVECTION to 375°F. Combine raisins, pecans, sugar, and cinnamon; reserve 1 tablespoon of mixture. Unroll and separate dough into eight triangles. Brush top surface of dough triangles with 1 table-spoon melted butter; sprinkle evenly with raisin mixture. Roll up according to package directions. Brush tops with remaining butter; sprinkle with reserved raisin mixture. Place rolls directly on ungreased turntable. Cook at CONVECTION (375°F) for 12 to 14 minutes or until lightly browned. Serve warm.

8 rolls

FRESH FRUIT COBBLER

3 cups assorted bite-size fresh fruit (blueberries, strawberries, peaches, etc.)

1 cup flour

1/2 cup sugar

1 teaspoon baking powder

2 eggs, beaten

1/4 cup milk

1/2 teaspoon vanilla extract

1/2 teaspoon grated fresh lemon rind

Place fruit in an 8×8×2-inch glass baking dish to make a 1-inch deep layer. Sift flour, sugar, and baking powder into a medium mixing bowl. Add eggs, milk, vanilla, and lemon rind; stir until batter is smooth. Pour batter over fruit; spread to cover. Cook at COMBI LOW for 35 to 37 minutes or until golden brown. Let stand 10 minutes.

8 servings

CARAMEL CUSTARD

1 cup sugar, divided

3 tablespoons water

2 cups milk

4 eggs, beaten

1/2 teaspoon vanilla extract

Combine 2/3 cup sugar and water in a 1-cup glass measuring cup. Cook uncovered at POWER HI for 5 1/2 to 6 minutes or until sugar is golden brown. Pour into six buttered 6-ounce glass custard cups; set aside. Pour milk into a 2-cup glass measuring cup. Cook uncovered at POWER HI for 4 minutes. Beat eggs, remaining sugar, and vanilla in a 1-quart glass measuring cup; gradually stir in milk. Pour over caramel in custard cups. Arrange in a circular pattern on turntable. Cook uncovered at POWER 5 for 9 to 10 minutes or until custard is set. Let stand until cool. Refrigerate covered for at least 3 hours before inverting to serve.

6 servings

PUMPKIN BREAD

1¼ cups flour

½ cup packed brown sugar

¼ cup sugar

2 teaspoons pumpkin pie spice

1 teaspoon baking powder

1 teaspoon baking soda

½ teaspoon salt

1 cup canned pumpkin

2 eggs

⅔ cup vegetable oil

⅓ cup finely chopped nuts

Preheat CONVECTION to 325°F. Combine flour, brown sugar, sugar, pie spice, baking powder, baking soda, salt, pumpkin, eggs, oil, and nuts in a large mixing bowl. Beat at low speed of electric mixer until ingredients are just moistened, scraping bowl occasionally. Spread batter evenly into a greased 8×4-inch metal pan. Cook at CONVECTION (325°F) for 45 to 50 minutes or until wooden pick inserted near center comes out clean. Cool 10 minutes; remove from pan. Cool completely before slicing.

1 loaf

PECAN AND RAISIN STUFFED APPLES

½ cup raisins

¼ cup packed brown sugar

¼ cup chopped pecans

2 tablespoons lemon juice

½ teaspoon cinnamon

¼ teaspoon ground nutmeg

4 large baking apples (about 2 pounds)

¼ cup butter or margarine

Combine raisins, brandy, brown sugar, pecans, lemon juice, cinnamon, and nutmeg in a 2-cup glass measuring cup. Cook uncovered at POWER HI for 1½ to 2 minutes or until hot; stir. Core apples and pare skin one-quarter of the way down. Fill centers of each apple with 2 tablespoons of raisin-nut mixture; top with 1 tablespoon butter. Place apples in an 8×8×2-inch glass baking dish. Cook uncovered at POWER HI for 10 to 12 minutes or until apples are tender.

4 servings

Beverages

MEXICAN COFFEE

¹/₄ cup heavy cream

2 teaspoons chocolate syrup

¹/₄ teaspoon cinnamon

³/₄ cup strong coffee or espresso, freshly brewed

3 tablespoons coffee-flavored liqueur

Whipped cream

Combine cream, chocolate syrup, and cinnamon in a 10-ounce microwavable mug. Stir in coffee. Cook uncovered at POWER 7 for 1 ½ to 2 minutes or until thoroughly heated. Stir in liqueur. Top with whipped cream. Serve immediately.

1 serving

HOT SPICED CIDER

3 cups apple cider

1 tablespoon packed brown sugar

1 piece (1-inch) cinnamon stick

1 teaspoon whole cloves

Combine cider, brown sugar, cinnamon stick, and cloves in a 1-quart glass measuring cup. Cook uncovered at POWER HI for 7 to 8 minutes or until cider boils. Let stand 1 to 2 minutes. Strain into serving mugs.

3 cups

WARMED SANGRIA

1 orange, thinly sliced

1 lemon, thinly sliced

¹/₄ cup brandy

2 tablespoons packed brown sugar

1 cinnamon stick

3 cups dry red wine

Combine orange, lemon, brandy, brown sugar, and cinnamon stick in a 2-quart glass measuring cup. Cook uncovered at POWER HI for 2 minutes. Stir in wine. Cook uncovered at POWER HI for 2 to 3 minutes or until wine is warmed. Remove cinnamon stick. Serve with sliced orange and lemon.

4 1/2 cups

Special Feature

See Use and Care manual for additional information on these special features.
AUTO WEIGHT COMBINATION COOKING

Auto Weight Combination programs will set the correct microwave power and oven temperature for you, and calculate cooking times.

Beef, pork, chicken, turkey, and lamb can be cooked on Auto Weight Combination. No power levels or times need to be set. Just weigh the item to be cooked and place on the cooking accessories.

To use, simply select the category by touching Combi Cook and number pad. Then enter the weight of your food in decimal increments from 0.1, to 5.9 pounds.
The oven will determine the cooking time and combination. Once you press "START" the cooking time will appear in the display.

The oven will sound the beep at the half of cooking time. At the beep, turn over and rearrange.

Note: If the oven door is not opened during the beep, the oven will continue to cook. Turning and rearranging are necessary for best results.

There are seven categories for Auto Weight Combination. Listed are the recommended foods and the maximum weights that can be cooked in each category. For proper cooking results on the Auto Weight Combination, let meat stand covered with foil 10 to 15 minutes after removing from oven.

Combination	Food	Maximum Weight	Accessory
1	BEEF-RARE	5.9 pounds	Rack
2	BEEF-MEDIUM	5.9 pounds	Rack
3	BEEF-WELL	5.9 pounds	Rack
4	LAMB-MEDIUM	5.9 pounds	Rack
5	LAMB-WELL	5.9 pounds	Rack
6	PORK	5.9 pounds	Rack
7	CHICKEN/TURKEY	5.9 pounds	Rack

AUTO WEIGHT DEFROST

To help you become throughly familiar with the convenient Auto Weight Defrost method and its use, we have provided step-by-step instructions for you.
You will soon see how microwave defrosting can transform defrosting from a time-consuming nuisance to a simple preparaton step. Let's begin by defrosting 1 pound 8 ounces of ground beef.

1. Unwrap beef and place on a microwavable roast rack or tray (to catch drippings). Set dish in the oven on the turntable.
2. Press CLEAR.
3. Ground beef defrosts on "MEAT". Press "MEAT". "DEF 1" will be shown, and the "lbs" light will be blinking.
4. Enter the weight of your food in decimal increments from 0.1 pound to 9.9 pounds. Remember to convert ounces to tenths of a pound. To defrost 1 pound 8 ounces of ground beef, touch number pads. "1" and "5" for 1.5 pounds. The display window will show "1.5".
5. Touch START. The oven will begin the defrosting sequence and the display window will show the total time as it "counts down". The oven will sound the beep at the end of first stage.
6. At the beep, follow the use and care manual instructions: Remove thawed portions with fork, turning beef over and also removing any thawed portion. Return remainder to oven. NOTE: If the oven door is not opened during the beep, the oven will continue to defrost. Because turning and separating are usually necessary for proper defrosting, follow steps 1 through 7 for best results.
7. After performing guide instructions, touch START. The oven resumes defrosting and the display window shows the time remaining. At the end of the required time, the beep will sound and "End" will appear in the display window for 2 seconds. The oven shuts off automatically.

AUTO WEIGHT DEFROST GUIDE-MEAT

Food	Setting	At Beep	Special Instructions
BEEF			Meat of irregular shape and large, fatty cuts of meat should have the narrow or fatty areas shielded with foil at the beginning of a defrost sequence.
Ground Beef (bulk)	MEAT	Remove thawed portions with fork. Turn over. Return remainder to oven.	Do not defrost less than ¼ lb. Freeze in doughnut shape.
Ground beef (patties)	MEAT	Separate and rearrange.	Do not defrost less than two 4-oz. patties. Depress center when freezing.
Hamburger patty	MEAT	Separate and rearrange.	Place on microwavable roast rack
Pot roast chuck roast	MEAT	Turn over. Cover warm areas with aluminum foil.	Place on microwavable roast rack.
Rib roast	MEAT	Turn over. Cover warm areas with aluminum foil.	Place on microwavable roast rack.
Rolled rump roast	MEAT	Turn over. Cover warm areas with aluminum foil.	Place on microwavable roast rack.
Round steak	MEAT	Turn over. Cover warm areas with aluminum foil.	Place on microwavable roast rack.
Stew beef	MEAT	Remove thawed portions with fork. Separate remainder. Return remainder to oven.	Place in microwavable baking dish.
Tenderloin Steak	MEAT	Turn over. Cover warm areas with aluminum foil.	Place on microwavable roast rack.
LAMB			
Chops (1-inch thick)	MEAT	Separate and rearrange.	Place on microwavable roast rack.
Cubes for stew	MEAT	Remove thawed portions with fork. Separate remainder. Return remainder to oven.	Place in microwavable baking dish.
Rolled roast.	MEAT	Turn over. Cover warm areas with aluminum foil.	Place on microwavable roast rack.
PORK			
Bacon	MEAT	Separate and rearrange.	Place on microwavable roast rack.
Chops (½-inch thick)	MEAT	Separate and rearrange.	Place on microwavable roast rack.
Country-style ribs	MEAT	Turn over. Cover warm areas with aluminum foil.	Place on microwavable roast rack.
Hot dogs	MEAT	Separate and rearrange.	Place on microwavable roast rack.
Rolled roast, boneless	MEAT	Turn over. Cover warm areas with alumiinum foil.	Place on microwavable roast rack.
Sausage bulk	MEAT	Remove thawed portions with fork. Turn over. Return remainder to oven.	Place in microwavable baking dish.
Sausage links	MEAT	Separate and rearrange.	Place on microwavable roast rack.
Spareribs	MEAT	Turn over. Cover warm areas with aluminum foil.	Place on microwavable roast rack.
VEAL			
Cutlets (1 lb., ½-inch thick)	MEAT	Separate and rearrange.	Place on microwavable roast rack.

AUTO WEIGHT DEFROST GUIDE-POULTRY

Food	Setting	At Beep	Special Instructions
CHICKEN			No poultry over 5.9 lbs. should be defrosted using AUTO DEFROST, nor should any whole turkeys be defrosted with this setting.
Breasts (boneless)	POULTRY	Separate and turn over. Cover with waxed paper.	Place on a microwavable roast rack. Finish defrosting by immersing in cold water.
Cut up	POULTRY	Separate pieces and rearrange. Turn over. Cover warm areas with aluminum foil.	Place on microwavable roast rack. Finish defrosting by immersing in cold water.
Whole (under 4 lbs.)	POULTRY	Turn over (breast-side down). Cover warm areas with aluminum foil.	Place chicken breast-side-up on microwavable roast rack. Finish defrosting by immersing in cold water. Remove giblet when chicken is partially defrosted.
CORNISH HENS Whole	POULTRY	Turn over. Cover warm areas with aluminum foil.	Place on microwavable roast rack. Finish defrosting by immersing in cold water.
TURKEY Breast (under 6 lbs.)	POULTRY	Turn over. Cover warm areas with aluminum foil.	Place on microwavable roast rack. Finish defrosting by immersing in cold water.

AUTO WEIGHT DEFROST GUIDE-FISH AND SHELLFISH

Food	Setting	At Beep	Special Instructions
FISH Fillets	FISH	Turn over. Separate fillets when Partially thawed.	Place in microwavable baking dish. Carefully separate fillets under cold running water.
Steaks	FISH	Separate and rearrange.	Place in microwavable baking dish. Finish defrosting under cold running water.
Whole	FISH	Turn over.	Place in microwavable baking dish. Cover head and taill with foil; do not let foil touch sides of microwavable. Finish defrosting by immersing in cold water.
SHELLFISH Crabmeat	FISH	Break apart. Turn over.	Place in microwavable baking dish.
Lobster tails	FISH	Turn over and rearrange.	Place in microwavable baking dish.
Shrimp	FISH	Break apart and rearrange.	Place in microwavable baking dish.
Scallops	FISH	Break apart and rearrange.	Place in microwavable baking dish.

Cooking Chart

MEAT COOKING CHART

Meat	Cooking Mode	Cooking Time	Special Instructions
BEEF Corned Beef (3 lbs.)	(Cook 1) MICRO POWER HI then (Cook 2) MICRO POWER 3	15 minutes 47 to 53 minutes per pound	Place corned beef in 3-quart microwavable casserole. Pour 1 cup of water and desired seasonings over corned beef. Cook covered. Turn over beef twice during cooking. Shield thinner ends with foil. Cook until fork-tender. Let stand covered 15 minutes. Thinly slice beef diagonally across grain.
Cubes for stew (2 lb. 1-inch cubes)	(Cook 1) MICRO POWER HI then (Cook 2) MICRO POWER 3	10 minutes 36 minutes per pound	Place cubes in 2½-quart microwavable casserole. Pour 1 cup of water or broth over cubes. Cook covered. Stir cubes halfway through cooking. Cook until fork-tender. Let stand covered 10 minutes.
Ground beef (1 lb.)	MICRO POWER HI	5 to 6 minutes	Crumble beef and place in microwavable sieve or colander. Place sieve in microwavable bowl to collect drippings. Cover with waxed paper. Stir after 3 minutes to break meat apart. After cooking let stand covered 2 minutes. If meat is still pink, cover and cook 1 more minute.
Hamburgers, Fresh or defrosted fro- zen(4 oz. each) 1 patty 2 patties 4 patties	COMBI HIGH	 9 to 10 minutes 9 to 10 minutes 11 to 12 minutes	Arrange patties on microwavable and ovenproof roast rack. Place roast rack or CONVECTION rack on turntable. Remove from oven and let stand 1 to 2 minutes.
Pot roast (3-4 lbs.)	(Cook 1) MICRO POWER HI then (Cook 2) MICRO POWER 3	15 minutes 42 to 47 minutes per pound	Pierce roast deeply on both sides in several places. Place roast in large cooking bag; place in microwavable dish. Add desired seasonings and 1 cup of liquid over roast. Close bag loosely with microwavable closure or string. Carefully turn meat over after 45 minutes. Continue cooking until fork-tender. Let stand in bag 10 minutes.
Rib roast, rolled (3-4 lbs.)	COMBI HIGH	11 to 13 minutes per pound, RARE (135°F) 13 to 16 minutes per pound, MEDIUM (155°F)	Place roast fat side down on microwavable and ovenproof roast rack. Add desired **seasonings** and place on CONVECTION rack on turntable. Shield if necessary. Remove from oven and let stand covered with foil 15 minutes. (Temperature may rise about 10°F)
Rump roast, rolled (3-4 lbs.)	COMBI LOW	20 to 22 minutes per pound, RARE (135°F) 23 to 25 minutes per pound, MEDIUM (155°F)	Place roast fat side down on microwavable and ovenproof roast rack. Add desired seasonings and place on CONVECTION rack on turntable. Shield if necessary. Remove from oven and let stand covered with foil 15 minutes (Temperature may rise about 10°F).

MEAT COOKING CHART (Cont'd)

Meat	Cooking Mode	Cooking Time	Special Instructions
Sirloin tip roast (3-4 lbs.)	COMBI HIGH	11 to 13 minutes per pound, RARE (135°F) 13 to 16 minutes per pound, MEDIUM (155°F)	Place roast fat side down on microwavable and ovenproof roast rack. Add desired seasonings and place on CONVECTION rack on turntable. Remove from oven and let stand covered with foil 15 minutes. (Temperature may rise about 10°F).
LAMB Lamb roast, rolled, boneless (3-4 lbs.)	COMBI HIGH	12 to 13 minutes per pound, RARE (135°F) 14 to 15 minutes per pound, MEDIUM (145°F) 16 to 16½ minutes per pound, WELL (155°F)	Place roast fat side down on microwavable and ovenproof roast rack. Brush with marinade and desired seasonings such as rosemary, thyme or marjoram. Place on CONVECTION rack on turntable. Remove from oven and let stand covered with foil 15 minutes. (Temperature may rise about 10°F).
Lamb stew cubes, (2 lbs.) 1-inch cubes	(Cook 1) MICRO POWER HI then (Cook 2) MICRO POWER 3	10 minutes 37 minutes per pound	Place cubes in 2-quart microwavable casserole. Add desired seasonings such as rosemary, thyme and marjoram and 1 cup of water. Cook covered. Stir cubes twice during cooking. Cook until fork tender. Let stand covered 15 minutes.
PORK Bacon slices 2 slices 4 slices 6 slices	MICRO POWER HI	1½ to 2 minutes 3 to 4 minutes 4½ to 5½ minutes	Place bacon slices on microwavable roast rack. Cover with microwavable paper towel. After cooking let stand covered 1 minute.
Canadian bacon 2 slices 4 slices 6 slices	MICRO POWER HI	30 to 45 seconds 1 to 1½ minutes 1 to 2 minutes	Place meat on microwavable roast rack. Cover loosely with waxed paper. After cooking let stand covered 1 minute.
Chops 2 chops (about 12 oz.) 4 chops (1½ lbs.)	COMBI LOW	16 to 19 minutes 30 to 35 minutes	Place chops in microwavable and ovenproof roast rack. Add desired seasonings and place on CONVECTION rack on turntable. Cook until no longer pink or until internal temperature reaches 170°F. Turn over chops halfway through cooking. Remove from oven and let stand covered 5 minutes. (Temperature may rise about 10°F).
Hot dogs 1 2 4	MICRO POWER HI	30 to 45 seconds 45 to 60 seconds 1 to 2 minutes	Pierce hot dogs and place on microwavable roast rack. Cover with waxed paper. If in bun wrap in microwavable paper towel or paper napkin to absorb moisture. After cooking, let stand 30 seconds to 1 minute.
Ham, boneless fully cooked 2 lbs. 5 lbs.	MICRO POWER 5	10 to 15 minutes per pound	Place ham on microwavable roast rack. Cover with waxed paper. Turn ham over halfway through cooking. Cook until internal temperature reaches 120°F. Let stand covered 10 minutes.

MEAT COOKING CHART (Cont'd)

Meat	Cooking Mode	Cooking Time	Special Instructions
Ham, center slice (1 lb.)	MICRO POWER 5	5 to 6 minutes	Place slice on microwavable roast rack. Cover with plastic wrap; vent. After cooking let stand covered 1 minute.
Loin roast, rolled, boneless (3½-4½ lbs.)	COMBI LOW	15 to 17 minutes per pound	Place roast on microwavable and ovenproof roast rack. Add desired seasonings and place on CONVECTION rack on turntable. After cooking remove from oven and let stand 15 minutes. (Temperature may rise about 10°F). Internal temperature of pork should reach 170°F before serving.
Sausage links, Fresh or defrosted frozen	CONVECTION 400°F	12 to 14 minutes	Preheat CONVECTION to 400°F. Pierce links and place on ovenproof roast rack. Turn links over halfway through cooking.
Sausage patties, Fresh (2 oz. each) 2 patties 4 patties 6 patties	CONVECTION 400°F	18 to 20 minutes	Place sausage patties on ovenproof roast rack. Turn patties over after 10 minutes of cooking.
Spareribs (2½-3½ lbs.)	MICRO POWER 5	27 to 32 minutes per pound (165°F)	Place ribs, cut into serving size pieces, bone side down in large cooking bag. Place bag in 3-quart microwavable casserole. Add 1 cup of water to bag. Close bag loosely with microwavable closure or string. Turn ribs over, rearranging carefully, halfway through cooking. Cook until meat is fork-tender. Carefully remove ribs.
	then MICRO POWER 5 (if desired)	10 minutes (if desired)	If desired, place ribs on microwavable roast rack and brush sauce over ribs. Cook covered with waxed paper. Let stand covered 10 minutes. (Temperature may rise about 10°F). Internal temperature of pork should reach 170°F before serving.

NOTE: Using oven mitts, or hot pads, carefully insert and remove turntable and CONVECTION rack together for ease in handing.

POULTRY COOKING CHART

Poultry	Cooking Mode	Cooking Time	Special Instructions
Chicken Breasts, boneless 1 half breast (4-5 oz.) 1 whole breast (10-12 oz.)	COMBI HIGH COMBI HIGH	6 to 8 minutes 15 to 17 minutes	Wash and dry poultry. Remove skin and place breasts, thickest portions to outside, on microwavable and ovenproof roast rack. Place on CONVECTION rack on turntable. Brush with butter and seasonings if desired. Cook until no longer pink and juices run clear. Remove from oven and let stand covered 3 minutes.
Cut up fryer (2½-3 lbs.)	COMBI HIGH	30 to 35 minutes	Wash and dry poultry. Arrange pieces on Microwavable and ovenproof roast rack with thickest pieces to the outside. Brush with butter and seasonings if desired. Place on CONVECTION rack on turntable. Cook until no longer pink and juices run clear. Remove from oven and let stand covered 5 minutes.
Whole (3-3½ lbs.)	COMBI HIGH	35 to 40 minutes	Wash and dry poultry. Place on microwavable and ovenproof roast rack. Brush with butter and seasonings if desired. Place on CONVECTION rack on turntable. Cook until no longer pink and juices run clear. Remove from oven and let stand covered with foil 10 minutes. (Temperature may rise about 10°F). Temperature in thigh should be about 175°F-185°F when done.
Cornish Hens Two whole (1-1½ lbs. each)	COMBI HIGH	35 to 40 minutes	Wash and dry poultry. Tie wings to body of hen and the legs to tail. Place hens breast side up on microwavable and ovenproof roast rack. Brush with butter and seasonings if desired. Place on CONVECTION rack on turntable. Remove and discard drippings and shield bone ends of drumsticks with foil halfway through cooking if needed. Cook until no longer pink and juices run clear. Remove from oven and let stand covered with foil 5 minutes. (Temperature may rise about 10°F). Temperature in breast should be 170°F before serving.
Turkey Breast, boneless (2-3 lbs.)	COMBI HIGH	20 to 25 minutes per pound	Place thawed turkey breast, on microwavable and ovenproof roast rack. Brush with butter and seasonings if desired. Place on CONVECTION rack on turntable. Cook until no longer pink and juices run clear. Remove from oven and let stand covered with foil 10 minutes. (Temperature may rise about 10°F). Temperature in breast should be 170°F before serving.

POULTRY COOKING CHART (Cont'd)

Poultry	Cooking Mode	Cooking Time	Special Instructions
Turkey Breast, whole bone-in (4-9 lbs.)	COMBI HIGH	10 to 11 minutes per pound	Wash and dry poultry. Place turkey breast, on microwavable and ovenproof roast rack. Brush with butter and seasonings if desired. Place on turntable. Remove and discard drippings halfway through cooking. Cook until no longer pink and juices run clear. Remove from oven and let stand covered with foil 10 minutes. (Temperature may rise about 10°F). Temperature in breast should be 170°F before serving.
Drumsticks (1½-2 lbs.)	COMBI HIGH	25 to 30 minutes	Wash and dry poultry. Place pieces with thickest portion to outside on microwavable and ovenproof roast rack. Brush with butter and seasoning if desired. Place on CONVECTION rack on turntable. Cook until no longer pink and juices run clear. Remove from oven and let stand covered with foil 5 minutes.

NOTE: Using oven mitts or hot pads, carefully insert and remove turntable and CONVECTION rack together for ease in handing.

FISH AND SHELLFISH COOKING CHART

Fish and Shellfish	Cooking Mode	Cooking Time Minutes per Pound	Special Instructions
Fish fillets	MICRO POWER HI	4 to 5 minutes	Arrange fish in a single layer with thickest portion toward outside edge of 1½-quart microwavable baking dish. Brush with melted butter and season, if desired. Cook covered with plastic wrap; vent. Let stand covered 2 minutes.
Fish steaks	MICRO POWER HI	4 to 5 minutes	
Whole fish	MICRO POWER 7	6 to 7 minutes	
Scallops, sea	MICRO POWER HI	3 to 4 minutes	Prepare as directed above, except stir halfway through cooking.
Shrimp, shelled	MICRO POWER HI	3 to 4 minutes	
Lobster tail	MICRO POWER HI	4 to 5 minutes	Cut hard shell down middle with knife. Grasp tail with both hands and open flat. Place flesh side up in 8 x 8 x 2-inch square glass baking dish. Cook covered with waxed paper. Let stand covered 2 minutes.

CONVENIENCE FOODS COOKING CHART

Convection cooking of convenience foods is similar to cooking in a conventional oven. Select items that fit conveniently on the turntable, such as an 8½-inch frozen pizza. Preheat convection to the desired temperature, and use metal cooking utensils. When cooking or baking these convenience foods, follow package directions for preparation and container. Due to the great variety of foods available, times given here are approximate. It is advisable to always check foods about 5 minutes before the minimum recommended time, and cook longer only if needed. Use oven mitts or handle to insert or removal items from oven.

Food	Size/WT.	Cooking Mode	Cooking Time	Special Instructions
Fried Chicken (frozen)	2 pounds	COMBINATION HIGH	15 minutes	Spread in single layer on metal round cookie tray.
Pizza (frozen)	13 ounces (8½-inch)	CONVECTION 400°F (preheated)	14-16 minutes	Cook on CONVECTION rack for crisper crust.
Brownies	About 13 ounces	CONVECTION 350°F (preheated)	23-26 minutes	Bake in 9-inch square pan.
Frozen Custard Pie	26 ounces	CONVECTION 425°F (preheated)	50-60 minutes	Cook in metal or ovenproof pan.
Cake Layers	18.25 ounces	CONVECTION 350°F (preheated)	45 minutes	Cook one layer at a time on turntable.
Applesauce Cake	18.25 ounces	CONVECTION 350°F (preheated)	40-45 minutes	Use metal 10-cup fluted tube pan.
Date Nut Bread	17 ounces	CONVECTION 350°F (preheated)	40 minutes	Cook in 9 × 5-inch metal loaf pan.
Frozen Bread Dough	16 ounces	CONVECTION 375°F (preheated)	25-30 minutes	Follow package directions for thawing dough. Bake in metal greased 8½ × 4½ × 2½-inch loaf pan.
Refrigerated Cookies	20 ounces	CONVECTION 350°F	8 to 9½ minutes	Bake six at a time on metal round cookie sheet.

VEGETABLE COOKING CHART

Vegetable	Preparation	Amount	Cooking Time at Power Control HI	Standing Time
artichokes, fresh	whole	4 (8 oz. ea.)	10-12 minutes	5 minutes
artichokes, frozen	hearts	9-oz. package	7-9 minutes	5 minutes
asparagus, fresh	1½-in. pieces	1 lb.	5-6 minutes	3 minutes
asparagus, frozen	whole spears	10-oz. package	6-8 minutes	3 minutes
beans, green or wax, fresh	1½-in. pieces	1 lb.	6-8 minutes	–
beans, green or wax. frozen	cut up	9-oz. package	6-8 minutes	3 minutes
beets, fresh	sliced	1½-2 lbs.	10-12 minutes	5 minutes
broccoli, fresh	spears	1 lb.	6-8 minutes	–
broccoli, frozen	whole or cut	10-oz. package	6½-8½ minutes	3 minutes
Brussels sprouts, fresh	whole	10-oz. tub	6-7 minutes	–
Brussels sprouts, frozen	whole	10-oz. package	7-9 minutes	3 minutes
cabbage, fresh	chopped	1 lb.	6-7 minutes	5 minutes
	wedges	1 lb.	7-9 minutes	5 minutes
carrots, fresh	½-in. slices	1 lb.	6-7 minutes	3 minutes
carrots, frozen	sliced	10-oz. package	5-7 minutes	3 minutes
cauliflower, fresh	flowerets	1 medium head	6½-8 minutes	3 minutes
	whole	1 medium head	10-16 minutes	5 minutes
cauliflower, frozen	flowerets	10-oz. package	5-7 minutes	3 minutes
celery, fresh	½-in. slices	1 lb.	10-12 minutes	5 minutes
corn, fresh	on cob, husked	4 ears	10-12 minutes	5 minutes
corn, frozen	on cob, husked	4 ears	11-13 minutes	5 minutes
	whole kernel	10-oz. package	4-5 minutes	3 minutes
eggplant, fresh	cubed	1 lb.	7-8 minutes	3 minutes
	whole, pierced	1-1¼ lbs.	5-8 minutes	5 minutes
leeks, fresh	whole, ends	1 lb.	8-10 minutes	5 minutes
lima beans, frozen	whole	10-oz. package	5-7 minutes	3 minutes
mixed vegetables, frozen	–	10-oz. package	6-8 minutes	3 minutes
mushrooms, fresh	sliced	1 lb.	4-5 minutes	3 minutes
okra, frozen	sliced	10-oz. package	5-7 minutes	5 minutes
onions, fresh	whole, peeled	8-10 small	11-15 minutes	5 minutes
peas, fresh	shelled	1 lb.	5-7 minutes	–
peas, frozen	shelled	10-oz. package	5-7 minutes	3 minutes
pea pods (snow peas), frozen	whole	6-oz. package	4½-6 minutes	–
peas and carrots	–	10-oz. package	5-7 minutes	3 minutes
peas, black-eyed, frozen	whole	10-oz. package	20-25 minutes	5 minutes
parsnips, fresh	cubed	1 lb.	8-10 minutes	5 minutes
potatoes, white or sweet,	whole	4 (6 oz. ea.)	8-10 minutes	3 minutes
fresh	whole	8 (6 oz. ea.)	14-17 minutes	5 minutes
rutabagas, fresh	cubed	4 cups	12-13 minutes	5 minutes
spinach, fresh	whole leaf	1 lb.	5-6 minutes	–
spinach, frozen	leaf or chopped	10-oz. package	6½-8 minutes	3 minutes
squash, summer, fresh	½-in. slices	1 lb.	6-7 minutes	3 minutes
squash, summer, frozen	sliced	10-oz. package	5-7 minutes	3 minutes
squash, winter, fresh	whole, pierced	1½ lbs.	10-12 minutes	5 minutes
squash, winter, frozen	whipped	12-oz. package	6-8 minutes	3 minutes
succotash, frozen	–	10-oz. package	5-7 minutes	3 minutes
turnips, fresh	cubed	4 cups	10-12 minutes	3 minutes

Index

Printed in Korea